Connected  Mathematics™

Shapes and Designs

Two-Dimensional Geometry

W9-AMW-347

Teacher's Edition

Glenda Lappan
James T. Fey
William M. Fitzgerald
Susan N. Friel
Elizabeth Difanis Phillips

Developed at Michigan State University

DALE SEYMOUR PUBLICATIONS®
MENLO PARK, CALIFORNIA

Connected Mathematics™ was developed at Michigan State University with the support of National Science Foundation Grant No. MDR 9150217.

This project was supported, in part, by the
National Science Foundation
Opinions expressed are those of the authors and not necessarily those of the Foundation

The Michigan State University authors and administration have agreed that all MSU royalties arising from this publication will be devoted to purposes supported by the Department of Mathematics and the MSU Mathematics Education Enrichment Fund.

This book is published by Dale Seymour Publications®, an imprint of Addison Wesley Longman, Inc.

Dale Seymour Publications
2725 Sand Hill Road
Menlo Park, CA 94025
Customer Service: 800 872-1100

Managing Editor: Catherine Anderson
Project Editor: Stacey Miceli
Book Editor: Mali Apple
ESL Consultant: Nancy Sokol Green
Revision Editor: James P. McAuliffe
Production/Manufacturing Director: Janet Yearian
Production/Manufacturing Coordinators: Claire Flaherty, Alan Noyes
Design Manager: John F. Kelly
Photo Editor: Roberta Spieckerman
Design: Don Taka
Composition: London Road Design, Palo Alto, CA
Electronic Prepress Revison: A. W. Kingston Publishing Services, Chandler, AZ
Illustrations: Pauline Phung, Margaret Copeland, Mitchell Rose, Ray Godfrey
Cover: Ray Godfrey

Photo Acknowledgements: 4 (belts) © M. Brodskaya/Bruce Coleman, Inc.; 4 (quilt) © Peter Southwick/Stock,Boston; 4 (sleeve bands) © Asian Art Museum of San Francisco/The Avery Brundage Collection; 4 (Dept. of Defense) © UPI/ Bettmann; 4 (National Gallery) © Peter Gridley/FPG International; 8 © Treat Davidson from National Audubon Society/ Photo Researchers, Inc.; 12 © Robert DiGiacomo/Comstock; 20 © Kerwin B. Roche/FPG International; 32 © ACME/UPI/ Bettmann; 64 (calendar) © The Bettmann Archives; 64 (basket) © B. Daemmrick/The Image Works; 65 © Michael Dwyer/Stock, Boston; 75 © (bicycle) Jerry Howard/Stock, Boston; 75 (window) © Tom Croke/Liason International; 75 (fan) © Ron Rovtar/FPG International; 75 (web) © Michael Siluk/The Image Works

DALE SEYMOUR PUBLICATIONS®

Order number 45820
ISBN 1-57232-625-5

4 5 6 7 8 9 10-ML-01 00

The Connected Mathematics Project Staff

Project Directors

James T. Fey
University of Maryland

William M. Fitzgerald
Michigan State University

Susan N. Friel
University of North Carolina at Chapel Hill

Glenda Lappan
Michigan State University

Elizabeth Difanis Phillips
Michigan State University

Project Manager

Kathy Burgis
Michigan State University

Technical Coordinator

Judith Martus Miller
Michigan State University

Collaborating Teachers/Writers

Mary K. Bouck
Portland, Michigan

Jacqueline Stewart
Okemos, Michigan

Curriculum Development Consultants

David Ben-Chaim
Weizmann Institute

Alex Friedlander
Weizmann Institute

Eleanor Geiger
University of Maryland

Jane Mitchell
University of North Carolina at Chapel Hill

Anthony D. Rickard
Alma College

Evaluation Team

Mark Hoover
Michigan State University

Diane V. Lambdin
Indiana University

Sandra K. Wilcox
Michigan State University

Judith S. Zawojewski
National-Louis University

Graduate Assistants

Scott J. Baldridge
Michigan State University

Angie S. Eshelman
Michigan State University

M. Faaiz Gierdien
Michigan State University

Jane M. Keiser
Indiana University

Angela S. Krebs
Michigan State University

James M. Larson
Michigan State University

Ronald Preston
Indiana University

Tat Ming Sze
Michigan State University

Sarah Theule-Lubienski
Michigan State University

Jeffrey J. Wanko
Michigan State University

Field Test Production Team

Katherine Oesterle
Michigan State University

Stacey L. Otto
University of North Carolina at Chapel Hill

Teacher/Assessment Team

Kathy Booth
Waverly, Michigan

Anita Clark
Marshall, Michigan

Theodore Gardella
Bloomfield Hills, Michigan

Yvonne Grant
Portland, Michigan

Linda R. Lobue
Vista, California

Suzanne McGrath
Chula Vista, California

Nancy McIntyre
Troy, Michigan

Linda Walker
Tallahassee, Florida

Software Developer

Richard Burgis
East Lansing, Michigan

Development Center Directors

Nicholas Branca
San Diego State University

Dianne Briars
Pittsburgh Public Schools

Frances R. Curcio
New York University

Perry Lanier
Michigan State University

J. Michael Shaughnessy
Portland State University

Charles Vonder Embse
Central Michigan University

Field Test Coordinators

Michelle Bohan
Queens, New York

Melanie Branca
San Diego, California

Alecia Devantier
Shepherd, Michigan

Jenny Jorgensen
Flint, Michigan

Sandra Kralovec
Portland, Oregon

Sonia Marsalis
Flint, Michigan

William Schaeffer
Pittsburgh, Pennsylvania

Karma Vince
Toledo, Ohio

Virginia Wolf
Pittsburgh, Pennsylvania

Shirel Yaloz
Queens, New York

Student Assistants

Laura Hammond
David Roche
Courtney Stoner
Jovan Trpovski
Julie Valicenti
Michigan State University

Advisory Board

Joseph Adney
Michigan State University (Emeritus)

Charles Allan
Michigan Department of Education

Mary K. Bouck
Portland Public Schools
Portland, Michigan

C. Stuart Brewster
Palo Alto, California

Anita Clark
Marshall Public Schools
Marshall, Michigan

David Doherty
GMI Engineering and Management Institute
Flint, Michigan

Kay Gilliland
EQUALS
Berkeley, California

David Green
GMI Engineering and Management Institute
Flint, Michigan

Henry Heikkinen
University of Northern Colorado
Greeley, Colorado

Anita Johnston
Jackson Community College
Jackson, Michigan

Elizabeth M. Jones
Lansing School District
Lansing, Michigan

Jim Landwehr
AT&T Bell Laboratories
Murray Hill, New Jersey

Peter Lappan
Michigan State University

Steven Leinwand
Connecticut Department of Education

Nancy McIntyre
Troy Public Schools
Troy, Michigan

Valerie Mills
Ypsilanti Public Schools
Ypsilanti, Michigan

David S. Moore
Purdue University
West Lafayette, Indiana

Ralph Oliva
Texas Instruments
Dallas, Texas

Richard Phillips
Michigan State University

Jacob Plotkin
Michigan State University

Dawn Pysarchik
Michigan State University

Rheta N. Rubenstein
University of Windsor
Windsor, Ontario, Canada

Susan Jo Russell
TERC
Cambridge, Massachusetts

Marjorie Senechal
Smith College
Northampton, Massachusetts

Sharon Senk
Michigan State University

Jacqueline Stewart
Okemos School District
Okemos, Michigan

Uri Treisman
University of Texas
Austin, Texas

Irvin E. Vance
Michigan State University

Linda Walker
Tallahassee Public Schools
Tallahassee, Florida

Gail Weeks
Northville Public Schools
Northville, Michigan

Pilot Teachers

California

National City

Laura Chavez
National City Middle School

Ruth Ann Duncan
National City Middle School

Sonia Nolla
National City Middle School

San Diego

James Ciolli
Los Altos Elementary School

Chula Vista

Agatha Graney
Hilltop Middle School

Suzanne McGrath
Eastlake Elementary School

Toni Miller
Hilltop Middle School

Lakeside

Eva Hollister
Tierra del Sol Middle School

Vista

Linda LoBue
Washington Middle School

Illinois

Evanston

Marlene Robinson
Baker Demonstration School

Michigan

Bloomfield Hills

Roxanne Cleveland
Bloomfield Hills Middle School

Constance Kelly
Bloomfield Hills Middle School

Tim Loula
Bloomfield Hills Middle School

Audrey Marsalese
Bloomfield Hills Middle School

Kara Reid
Bloomfield Hills Middle School

Joann Schultz
Bloomfield Hills Middle School

Flint

Joshua Coty
Holmes Middle School

Brenda Duckett-Jones
Brownell Elementary School

Lisa Earl
Holmes Middle School

Anne Heidel
Holmes Middle School

Chad Meyers
Brownell Elementary School

Greg Mickelson
Holmes Middle School

Rebecca Ray
Holmes Middle School

Patricia Wagner
Holmes Middle School

Greg Williams
Gundry Elementary School

Lansing

Susan Bissonette
Waverly Middle School

Kathy Booth
Waverly East Intermediate School

Carole Campbell
Waverly East Intermediate School

Gary Gillespie
Waverly East Intermediate School

Denise Kehren
Waverly Middle School

Virginia Larson
Waverly East Intermediate School

Kelly Martin
Waverly Middle School

Laurie Metevier
Waverly East Intermediate School

Craig Paksi
Waverly East Intermediate School

Tony Pecoraro
Waverly Middle School

Helene Rewa
Waverly East Intermediate School

Arnold Stiefel
Waverly Middle School

Portland

Bill Carlton
Portland Middle School

Kathy Dole
Portland Middle School

Debby Flate
Portland Middle School

Yvonne Grant
Portland Middle School

Terry Keusch
Portland Middle School

John Manzini
Portland Middle School

Mary Parker
Portland Middle School

Scott Sandborn
Portland Middle School

Shepherd

Steve Brant
Shepherd Middle School

Marty Brock
Shepherd Middle School

Cathy Church
Shepherd Middle School

Ginny Crandall
Shepherd Middle School

Craig Ericksen
Shepherd Middle School

Natalie Hackney
Shepherd Middle School

Bill Hamilton
Shepherd Middle School

Julie Salisbury
Shepherd Middle School

Sturgis

Sandra Allen
Eastwood Elementary School

Margaret Baker
Eastwood Elementary School

Steven Baker
Eastwood Elementary School

Keith Barnes
Sturgis Middle School

Wilodean Beckwith
Eastwood Elementary School

Darcy Bird
Eastwood Elementary School

Bill Dickey
Sturgis Middle School

Ellen Eisele
Sturgis Middle School

James Hoelscher
Sturgis Middle School

Richard Nolan
Sturgis Middle School

J. Hunter Raiford
Sturgis Middle School

Cindy Sprowl
Eastwood Elementary School

Leslie Stewart
Eastwood Elementary School

Connie Sutton
Eastwood Elementary School

Traverse City

Maureen Bauer
Interlochen Elementary School

Ivanka Berskshire
East Junior High School

Sarah Boehm
Courtade Elementary School

Marilyn Conklin
Interlochen Elementary School

Nancy Crandall
Blair Elementary School

Fran Cullen
Courtade Elementary School

Eric Dreier
Old Mission Elementary School

Lisa Dzierwa
Cherry Knoll Elementary School

Ray Fouch
West Junior High School

Ed Hargis
Willow Hill Elementary School

Richard Henry
West Junior High School

Dessie Hughes
Cherry Knoll Elementary School

Ruthanne Kladder
Oak Park Elementary School

Bonnie Knapp
West Junior High School

Sue Laisure
Sabin Elementary School

Stan Malaski
Oak Park Elementary School

Jody Meyers
Sabin Elementary School

Marsha Myles
East Junior High School

Mary Beth O'Neil
Traverse Heights Elementary School

Jan Palkowski
East Junior High School

Karen Richardson
Old Mission Elementary School

Kristin Sak
Bertha Vos Elementary School

Mary Beth Schmitt
East Junior High School

Mike Schrotenboer
Norris Elementary School

Gail Smith
Willow Hill Elementary School

Karrie Tufts
Eastern Elementary School

Mike Wilson
East Junior High School

Tom Wilson
West Junior High School

Minnesota

Minneapolis

Betsy Ford
Northeast Middle School

New York

East Elmhurst

Allison Clark
Louis Armstrong Middle School

Dorothy Hershey
Louis Armstrong Middle School

J. Lewis McNeece
Louis Armstrong Middle School

Rossana Perez
Louis Armstrong Middle School

Merna Porter
Louis Armstrong Middle School

Marie Turini
Louis Armstrong Middle School

North Carolina

Durham

Everly Broadway
Durham Public Schools

Thomas Carson
Duke School for Children

Mary Hebrank
Duke School for Children

Bill O'Connor
Duke School for Children

Ruth Pershing
Duke School for Children

Peter Reichert
Duke School for Children

Elizabeth City

Rita Banks
Elizabeth City Middle School

Beth Chaundry
Elizabeth City Middle School

Amy Cuthbertson
Elizabeth City Middle School

Deni Dennison
Elizabeth City Middle School

Jean Gray
Elizabeth City Middle School

John McMenamin
Elizabeth City Middle School

Nicollette Nixon
Elizabeth City Middle School

Malinda Norfleet
Elizabeth City Middle School

Joyce O'Neal
Elizabeth City Middle School

Clevie Sawyer
Elizabeth City Middle School

Juanita Shannon
Elizabeth City Middle School

Terry Thorne
Elizabeth City Middle School

Rebecca Wardour
Elizabeth City Middle School

Leora Winslow
Elizabeth City Middle School

Franklinton

Susan Haywood
Franklinton Elementary School

Clyde Melton
Franklinton Elementary School

Louisburg

Lisa Anderson
Terrell Lane Middle School

Jackie Frazier
Terrell Lane Middle School

Pam Harris
Terrell Lane Middle School

Ohio

Toledo

Bonnie Bias
Hawkins Elementary School

Marsha Jackish
Hawkins Elementary School

Lee Jagodzinski
DeVeaux Junior High School

Norma J. King
Old Orchard Elementary School

Margaret McCready
Old Orchard Elementary School

Carmella Morton
DeVeaux Junior High School

Karen C. Rohrs
Hawkins Elementary School

Marie Sahloff
DeVeaux Junior High School

L. Michael Vince
McTigue Junior High School

Brenda D. Watkins
Old Orchard Elementary School

Oregon

Portland

Roberta Cohen
Catlin Gabel School

David Ellenberg
Catlin Gabel School

Sara Normington
Catlin Gabel School

Karen Scholte-Arce
Catlin Gabel School

West Linn

Marge Burack
Wood Middle School

Tracy Wygant
Athey Creek Middle School

Canby

Sandra Kralovec
Ackerman Middle School

Pennsylvania

Pittsburgh

Sheryl Adams
Reizenstein Middle School

Sue Barie
Frick International Studies Academy

Suzie Berry
Frick International Studies Academy

Richard Delgrosso
Frick International Studies Academy

Janet Falkowski
Frick International Studies Academy

Joanne George
Reizenstein Middle School

Harriet Hopper
Reizenstein Middle School

Chuck Jessen
Reizenstein Middle School

Ken Labuskes
Reizenstein Middle School

Barbara Lewis
Reizenstein Middle School

Sharon Mihalich
Reizenstein Middle School

Marianne O'Connor
Frick International Studies Academy

Mark Sammartino
Reizenstein Middle School

Washington

Seattle

Chris Johnson
University Preparatory Academy

Rick Purn
University Preparatory Academy

Contents

Shapes are essential to the underlying structure of the landscapes and buildings in which we live and work, the furnishings in those spaces, and the tools and machines we use to create the things that are integral to our daily lives. Shapes also provide decoration for spaces and objects and the basis for creative artistic expressions of emotions and ideas.

Shapes and Designs is the first unit in the geometry strand that will develop students' ability to recognize, display, analyze, measure, and reason about the shapes and visual patterns that are such important features of our world. It builds on students' elementary-school exposure to simple shapes to begin analyzing the properties that make certain shapes special. The unit focuses on polygons and on the side and angle relationships of regular and irregular polygons (circles and other curves are explored in later units).

The introduction to *Shapes and Designs* in the student edition develops the broad theme of the unit: Of the shapes we use as basic components in the structures we design and build and in the art we create, some simple figures occur again and again because of properties that make them especially attractive and useful. The goal of *Shapes and Designs* is to have students discover and analyze many of the key properties of polygonal shapes that make them useful and attractive. As students become observant of the multitude of shapes that surround them and aware of the reasons that shapes are used for specific purposes, they will be amazed by the visual pleasure and practical insights their new knowledge provides. We suspect that teachers will share this eye-opening experience, finding new signs of beauty and structural significance in the things they see every day.

The approach to geometry in this unit is somewhat unique. First, the primary focus of the unit is on *recognition of properties of shapes* that have important practical and aesthetic implications, not on simple classification and naming of figures. While some attention is given to naming familiar figures, each investigation focuses on particular key properties of figures and the importance of those properties in applications. For example, students are periodically asked to identify differences between squares, rectangles that are not squares, and parallelograms that are not rectangles. However, we do not stress the fact that all squares are rectangles and that all rectangles are parallelograms. Furthermore, we use a few special names for types of quadrilaterals (square, rectangle, and parallelogram), but not the arcane vocabulary (obtuse, acute, scalene) often used to sort triangles. We frequently ask students to find and describe places where they see polygons of particular types and to puzzle over why those particular shapes are used.

Geometry is a vast subject, rich with both simple visual patterns and subtle and complex shapes. To develop ideas related to the major theme—Why do things have the shapes that they do?—this unit focuses on polygons and develops two basic sub themes: How do the lengths of sides in a polygon determine its possible shapes and uses? and, How do the measures of angles in a polygon determine its possible shapes and uses?

The overall goal of *Shapes and Designs* is to have students discover patterns and regularities in the relations among sides and angles of basic polygons and to understand how those patterns can be helpful in using polygonal shapes to create interesting designs and useful structures. We assume students have had some prior exposure to the basic shapes and some of their names. However, the development in this unit is based on the van Hiele theory of geometry learning: we begin with *recognition* of shapes, then move to *classification* of shapes, and then to *analysis* of properties of those shapes. The overall development progresses from tactile and visual experiences to more general and abstract reasoning.

The first big question presented in *Shapes and Designs* to motivate analysis of polygons is the problem of *tiling* or *tessellating* a flat surface, or plane. What sorts of figures can be used to cover a surface without gaps or overlaps? Why do triangles, squares, rectangles, and hexagons work so well, while many other shapes are more problematic? The key, discovered early in the unit and finally proven at the close of the unit, is that among the *regular polygons* (polygons with all sides the same length and all angles the same measure), only equilateral triangles, squares, and regular hexagons will tile the plane. Many other figures—and combinations of figures—can be used to tile the plane, and when one understands the important properties of simple polygons, one can create an abundance of aesthetically appealing tiling patterns, complete with artistic embellishments in the style of artist M. C. Escher. However, *it is the discovery of what important properties of the figures make the tiling possible*—not the tiling question itself—that is the focus of the unit.

The question of tiling—introduced to students by the puzzle of why honeycombs are covered with hexagons—leads to a general consideration of how combinations of side lengths influence the shape of a polygon. Explorations with manipulatives will lead students to discover relationships among sides and shapes of triangles, quadrilaterals, and other polygons. Their explorations will have two critical results. First, they will discover the *triangle inequality*: the general principle that the combined lengths of two sides of any triangle will always exceed the length of the third side (if not, a triangle cannot be formed). Second, students will uncover the principle that there is only one triangular shape that can be made from three given sides, whereas for four given sides, there are many possible quadrilateral shapes. This second principle explains the extensive use of triangular bracing in buildings: once three sides have been fitted together, they form a stable figure. A quadrilateral, however, can be distorted into many other quadrilateral shapes, and can undergo total collapse much more easily than a triangle.

Students then explore angles in more depth, beginning from the fact that, except in the case of triangles, specifying side lengths is not sufficient to determine the shape of a polygon. The shape of a polygon is linked to the measures of angles formed where its sides meet. Work is done to relate angles to right angles, focusing on developing students' estimation skills with angles. The need for more precision leads to the introduction of a new measuring tool, the *goniometer* (gō´-nē-om´-i-ter) or *angle ruler.* All the preceding discoveries are pulled together in explorations that reveal the patterns of interior angles in regular polygons and the answer to the question, Which regular polygons can be used to tile the plane and why? The answer depends on the fundamental principle that angles surrounding a vertex point in a tiling must have measures adding to 360°. By looking at examples organized in a table, students determine the measure of each angle in a regular polygon with *n* sides. The unit ends with a short investigation involving Logo computer programming.

In assessing student learning of the *Shapes and Designs* unit, it is critical to employ something other than the typical "name that figure" or "measure that angle" type of question. Students should be asked to demonstrate that they know and understand basic side-angle relationships of various parallelograms by using *reasoning* to make inferences from given information. They should be asked to *estimate* the sizes of given angles and to sketch angles of given sizes. They should be able to explain some practical situations that embody the key properties of simple polygons. The aim of this unit is as much to get students looking at the world around them as it is to have them memorize facts about that world.

In geometry we often need to refer to a particular shape from among several that are given. We also need to be able to refer to a particular vertex or side of a figure. Several useful labeling schemes are frequently used in mathematics. Sometimes each vertex of a figure is labeled with a letter or number; sometimes we only need to distinguish a shape from among a set of shapes, so a single letter or number will suffice. Students need to develop flexibility in "reading" shapes and in using labeling schemes as a way to make their ideas about figures clear.

Mathematical and Problem-Solving Goals

Shapes and Designs was created to help students

- Acquire knowledge of some important properties of polygons and a general ability to recognize those shapes and their properties both in and out of the classroom
- Describe decorative and structural applications in which polygons of various shapes appear
- Hypothesize about why hexagonal shapes appear on the surface of honeycombs
- Explain the property of the triangle that makes it useful as a stable structure
- Explain the side and angle relationships that make parallelograms useful for designs and for structures like windows, doors, and tilings
- Estimate the size of any angle using reference to a right angle and other benchmark angles
- Use an angle ruler for making more accurate angle measurements
- Develop a variety of strategies—such as testing many different cases and looking for patterns in the results, finding extreme cases, and organizing results in a systematic way (e.g., so patterns are revealed)—for solving problems involving polygons and their properties

The overall goal of Connected Mathematics is to help students develop sound mathematical habits. Through their work in this and other geometry units, students learn important questions to ask themselves about any situation that can be represented and modeled mathematically, such as: *What kind of tiles will cover a flat surface? What do these tile shapes have in common? What geometric characteristic lets them fit together? What are the simplest geometric shapes and figures? How do these simple figures work together to make more complex shapes? How can angle measures be estimated? How much accuracy is needed? When is it important to find accurate angle measures? When can a circular grid be the basis for a graph? What patterns can be found in the angle measures of regular figures? Of non-regular figures? Do these patterns apply to other figures?*

Investigation 1: Bees and Polygons

This investigation poses the key question, What tile shapes can be used to cover the plane? It asks students to make conjectures about why honeycombs are covered with hexagons and to use physical materials to explore other possibilities.

Investigation 2: Building Polygons

This investigation is based on the general question, Is the shape of a polygon determined exactly by the lengths of its sides and the order in which those sides are connected? The three problems involve the use of manipulatives called *Polystrips*.

Investigation 3: Polygons and Angles

This investigation introduces three basic ways of thinking about angles and the ideas behind angle measurement. It gives students practice in estimating angle measurements based on a right angle. A measuring device—the angle ruler—is introduced, allowing more precise measures of angles. Students then explore a problem that looks at the possible consequences of making measurement errors.

Investigation 4: Polygon Properties and Tiling

This investigation focuses attention on some basic properties of familiar quadrilaterals, using tiling as a context.

Investigation 5: Side-Angle-Shape Connections

In this investigation, students look at what remains constant—and what changes—as triangles, squares, rectangles, and parallelograms are rotated and flipped. The symmetries of the figures become more evident as students work with them.

Investigation 6: Turtle Tracks

In this investigation, students use the Logo programming language to create computer designs. Two of the three problems in this investigation can be done even if students do not have access to computers.

Connections to Other Units

The ideas in *Shapes and Designs* build on and connect to several big ideas in other Connected Mathematics units.

Big Idea	Prior Work	Future Work
understanding parts of polygons and how parts of polygons are related	developing mathematical reasoning by analyzing integers and data (*Prime Time, Data About Us*); developing shape recognition skills (*elementary school*)	finding area and perimeter of 2-D figures (*Covering and Surrounding*); studying properties of 3-D cube figures (*Ruins of Montarek*); exploring similarity of 2-D figures (*Stretching and Shrinking*); finding surface area and volume of 3-D figures (*Filling and Wrapping*)
learning important properties of polygons	developing classification skills through classifying integers (e.g., even, odd, abundant, deficient) and data (e.g., categorical or numerical) (*Prime Time, Data About Us*); developing shape recognition skills (*elementary school*)	learning important properties of rectangles, triangles, and parallelograms (*Covering and Surrounding*); studying properties of 3-D cube figures (*Ruins of Montarek*); enlarging, shrinking, and distorting 2-D shapes (*Stretching and Shrinking*); learning properties of 3-D figures (*Filling and Wrapping*); learning and applying the Pythagorean Theorem (*Looking for Pythagoras*)
creating tilings with polygons and determining the properties of shapes that can be used to tile a surface	exploring how 2-D shapes fit together (*elementary school*)	understanding area as the exact number of square units needed to cover a 2-D figure (*Covering and Surrounding*); subdividing figures into similar figures (*Stretching and Shrinking*); connecting tessellations to isometries (*Kaleidoscopes, Hubcaps, and Mirrors*)
exploring symmetries in squares, rectangles, parallelograms, and equilateral triangles	exploring symmetry informally by looking at shapes of data sets (*Data Around Us*)	identifying symmetry in 3-D cubic figures (*Ruins of Montarek*); connecting symmetry to isometries (*Kaleidoscopes, Hubcaps, and Mirrors*)
programming in Logo	exploring and playing with computer programs and computer games	continuing to program in Logo (*Covering and Surrounding; Stretching and Shrinking; Kaleidoscopes, Hubcaps, and Mirrors*), working with graphing calculators (*Variables and Patterns; Moving Straight Ahead; Thinking with Mathematical Models; Frogs, Fleas, and Painted Cubes; Say It with Symbols*)

Materials

For students

■ Labsheets

■ Calculators

■ ShapeSet™ (1 per group; see "Manipulatives" below)

■ Polystrips (1 set per group; see "Manipulatives" below)

■ Brass fasteners

■ Number cubes (3 per group; optional)

■ Straightedges (rulers or strips of tag board)

■ Angle rulers

■ Isometric dot paper (provided as a blackline master)

■ Large sheets of unlined paper (for groups to record answers)

■ Colored pens, pencils, or markers

■ Scissors

■ Macintosh computer with *Turtle Math* software (optional; 1 for every 2–4 students; see "Technology" on the next page)

■ Blank sheets of transparency film and transparency markers (optional)

For the teacher

■ Transparencies and transparency markers (optional)

■ ShapeSet for use on the overhead projector (copy the blackline masters onto transparency film)

■ Polystrips

■ Brass fasteners

■ Macintosh computer with *Turtle Math* software (optional)

Manipulatives

The investigations in this unit use the ShapeSet and Polystrips, which are available through Dale Seymour Publications®. If you do not have these manipulatives, you can make them by using the blackline masters provided.

The ShapeSet

The ShapeSet is a set of polygons that students can use in this unit to explore sides, angles, and tilings. Each set contains enough shapes for a group of four students. If you do not have ShapeSets, you can make them by copying the blackline masters provided onto sheets of paper and cutting out the shapes. A ShapeSet consists of 16 copies of shapes A and B and 8 copies of each of the remaining polygons.

Polystrips

Polystrips are strips of plastic that can be pieced together with brass fasteners to form polygons. If you do not have Polystrips, you can make them by using the blackline masters provided. Copy the masters onto transparency film, cut out the strips, and punch the holes. Use brass fast to piece the strips together. Each group should have 6 strips of each length.

Technology

Connected Mathematics was developed with the belief that calculators should always be available and that students should decide when to use them. For this reason, we do not designate specific problems as "calculator problems." The calculations in *Shapes and Designs* involve only simple arithmetic, so nonscientific calculators are adequate.

Investigation 6 was written for use with *Turtle Math*, a version of the Logo computer language. *Turtle Math* runs on a Macintosh (system requirements: model LC or better, System 7 or later, minimum of 4 MB RAM). However, the problems in the investigation can be easily adapted for use with other Logo software packages running on either Macintosh or IBM-compatible computers. Ideally, Investigation 6 should be done with one computer per two to four students. However, because the learning payoff of the investigation is significant, it is recommended that you do this investigation even if you have only one computer that you can use for demonstration.

Resources

A wide variety of books on architecture and design will give insight into the historical and cultural richness of shapes and designs. In several places in the unit, you can connect the mathematics material with work of other disciplines. Artists and workers in the construction crafts could be exciting guest speakers for your class.

For students

Anno, Mitsumasa. *Anno's Math Games III.* New York: Philomel Books, 1991.
Burns, Marilyn. *The Greedy Triangle.* New York: Scholastic, 1994.
Friedman, Aileen. *A Cloak for a Dreamer.* New York: Scholastic, 1994.

For teachers

The two ideas in this unit most likely to be unfamiliar to teachers are tilings (also called tessellations) and the Logo programming language. Many teacher references are available; we have mentioned just a few here, along with one resource about the angle ruler.

Battista, Michael T. and Douglas H. Clements. "A Case for a Logo-based Elementary School Geometry Curriculum." *Arithmetic Teacher* (November 1988): 11–17. This article includes an extensive bibliography related to geometry and Logo.

Battista, Michael T. and Douglas H. Clements. "Constructing Geometric Concepts in Logo." *Arithmetic Teacher* (November 1990): 15–17.

Giganti, Paul Jr. and Mary Jo Cittadino. "The Art of Tessellation." *Arithmetic Teacher* (March 1990): 6–16. This article includes an extensive bibliography of related work.

Papert, Seymour. *Mindstorms: Children, Computers, and Powerful Ideas.* New York: Basic Books, Inc., 1980.

Rubenstein, Rheta N., Glenda Lappan, Elizabeth Phillips, and William Fitzgerald. "Angle Sense: A Valuable Connector." *Arithmetic Teacher* (February 1993): 352–358. This article includes an interesting discussion of the use of the angle ruler.

Seymour, Dale and Jill Britton. *Introduction to Tessellations.* Palo Alto, Calif.: Dale Seymour Publications, 1989.

TesselMania!. MECC, 6160 Summit Drive N, Minneapolis, MN 55430. This wonderful software program makes it easy for students to create their own tessellations on the computer.

Pacing Chart

This pacing chart gives estimates of the class time required for each investigation and assessment piece. Shaded rows indicate opportunities for assessment.

Investigations and Assessments	Class Time
1 Bees and Polygons	2 days
2 Building Polygons	3 days
3 Polygons and Angles	5 days
Check-Up 1	1/2 day
4 Polygon Properties and Tiling	3 days
5 Side-Angle-Shape Connections	2 days
Check-Up 2	1/2 day
6 Turtle Tracks	3 days
Quiz	1 day
Self-Assessment	Take home
Unit Test	1 day
The Unit Project	Take home

Vocabulary

The following words and concepts are introduced and used in *Shapes and Designs*. Concepts in the left column are those that are essential for student understanding of this and future units. The Descriptive Glossary gives descriptions of many of these words.

Essential	**Nonessential**
angle	angle ruler
degree	benchmark
hexagon	central angle
octagon	decagon
parallelogram	diagonal
pentagon	equilateral triangle
polygon	heptagon
quadrilateral	interior angle
rectangle	irregular polygon
regular polygon	isosceles triangle
right angle	line symmetry
side	property
square	tiling
symmetry	trapezoid
triangle	turn symmetry
vertex	wedge

Assessment Summary

Embedded Assessment

Opportunities for informal assessment of student progress are embedded throughout *Shapes and Designs* in the problems, the ACE questions, and Mathematical Reflections. Suggestions for observing as students discover and explore mathematical ideas, for probing to guide their progress in developing concepts and skills, and for questioning to determine their level of understanding can be found in the *Launch, Explore*, or *Summarize* sections of all investigation problems. Some examples:

- Investigation 4, Problem 4.1 *Launch* (page 50a) provides questions you might ask to determine whether your students can make informal observations about the sizes of the interior angles of polygons without measuring tools, and suggests a way you might help students who are struggling.

- Investigation 2, Problem 2.2 *Explore* (page 21d) explains how you might guide students to see that more than one quadrilateral can be built with a given set of side lengths.

- Investigation 3, Problem 3.5 *Summarize* (page 41g) suggests a demonstration you might do to help your students understand and describe turn symmetries.

ACE Assignments

An ACE (Applications—Connections—Extensions) section appears at the end of each investigation. To help you assign ACE questions, a list of assignment choices is given in the margin next to the reduced student page for each problem. Each list indicates the ACE questions that students should be able to answer after they complete the problem.

Partner Quiz

One quiz, which may be given after Investigation 6, is provided with *Shapes and Designs*. This quiz is designed to be completed by pairs of students with the opportunity for revision based on teacher feedback. You will find the quiz and its answers in the Assessment Resources section. As an alternative to the quiz provided, you can construct your own quizzes by combining questions from the Question Bank, the quiz, and unassigned ACE questions.

Check-Ups

Two check-ups, which may be given after Investigations 3 and 5, are provided for use as quick quizzes or as warm-up activities. Check-ups are designed for students to complete individually. You will find the check-ups and their answer keys in the Assessment Resources section.

Question Bank

A Question Bank provides questions you can use for homework, reviews, or quizzes. You will find the Question Bank and its answer key in the Assessment Resources section.

Notebook/Journal

Students should have notebooks to record and organize their work. In the notebooks will be their journals along with sections for vocabulary, homework, and quizzes and check-ups. In their journals, students can take notes, solve investigation problems, jot down ideas for their projects, and record their mathematical reflections. You should assess student journals for completeness rather than correctness; journals should be seen as "safe" places where students can try out their thinking. A Notebook Checklist and a Self-Assessment are provided in the Assessment Resources section. The Notebook Checklist helps students organize their notebooks. The Self-Assessment guides students as they review their notebooks to determine which ideas they have mastered and which ideas they still need to work on.

The Unit Project: What I Know About Shapes and Designs

As a final assessment in *Shapes and Designs*, you may administer the Unit Test or assign the Unit Project, My Special Number. The project is introduced at the beginning of the unit, when students are asked to begin collecting drawings, photos, and magazine clippings that show examples of shapes being used in the world around them. As students complete the investigations, they write new information about shapes and their properties in their journals. The project is formally introduced at the end of the unit. Students are asked to use all the concepts they have learned in *Shapes and Designs* to create a final project that shows everything they have learned about shapes and designs. A scoring rubric and samples of student work are given in the Assessment Resources section.

The Unit Test

As a final assessment in *Shapes and Designs*, you may assign the Unit Project or administer the Unit Test. The Unit Test focuses on the properties of polygons.

Introducing Your Students to *Shapes and Designs*

This introduction will set the tone for the kind of discussions that will take place in *Shapes and Designs*.

To begin the unit, you might have students brainstorm about shapes they see in the classroom and shapes they recall from outside the classroom. You could focus their attention on certain shapes that occur frequently, such as triangles and rectangles. This should give you an informal indication of how familiar students are with shapes and their names. Slides or photographs of interesting bridges, buildings, works of art, and other structures and objects in which shapes are commonly found can hook students into looking for shapes and designs in their environment. An exceptional set of geometry slides, called *Geometry in Our World*,[1] would also provide an excellent visual introduction.

The discussion of shapes that occur in the environment will flow naturally into a consideration of the important question of the unit: Why do

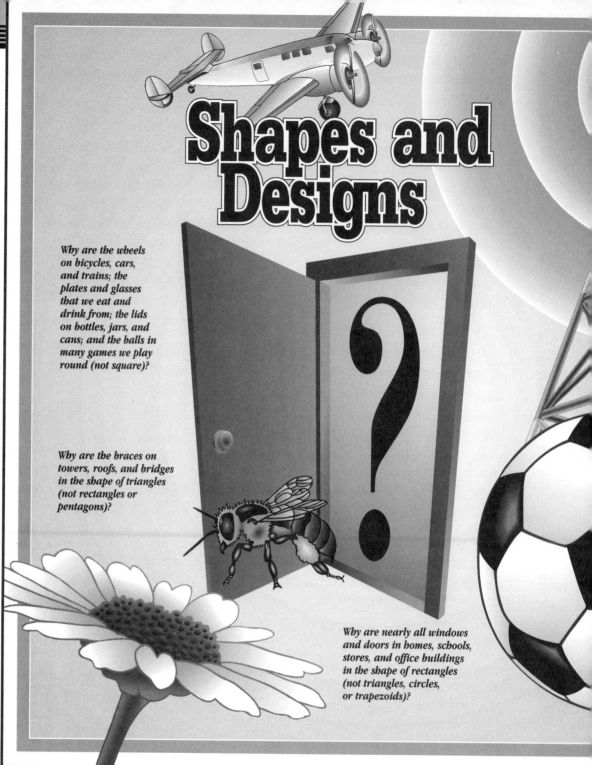

Shapes and Designs

Why are the wheels on bicycles, cars, and trains; the plates and glasses that we eat and drink from; the lids on bottles, jars, and cans; and the balls in many games we play round (not square)?

Why are the braces on towers, roofs, and bridges in the shape of triangles (not rectangles or pentagons)?

Why are nearly all windows and doors in homes, schools, stores, and office buildings in the shape of rectangles (not triangles, circles, or trapezoids)?

[1]Available from NCTM, 1906 Association Drive, Reston, VA 22091.

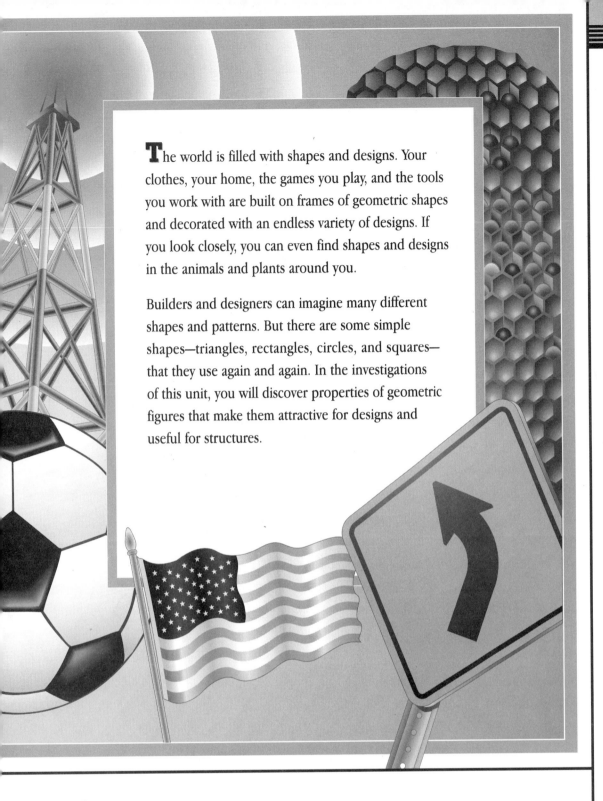

The world is filled with shapes and designs. Your clothes, your home, the games you play, and the tools you work with are built on frames of geometric shapes and decorated with an endless variety of designs. If you look closely, you can even find shapes and designs in the animals and plants around you.

Builders and designers can imagine many different shapes and patterns. But there are some simple shapes—triangles, rectangles, circles, and squares—that they use again and again. In the investigations of this unit, you will discover properties of geometric figures that make them attractive for designs and useful for structures.

certain shapes appear again and again in structures, nature, and works of art? Ask your students to think about the three questions posed on page 2 of the student edition. You may want to spend some time discussing answers to these questions. Rather than trying to get the best answers now, ask students to continue to think about these questions as they work through the unit. Each question is posed again in this unit when students have learned the mathematics involved in answering it. The question about rectangles appears again as ACE question 5 of Investigation 5. The question about circles is ACE question 44 of Investigation 3. The question about triangles is ACE question 14 of Investigation 2.

Polygons are the major focus of this unit. The student edition defines *polygons* as simple closed figures with straight-line sides that all lie in the same plane. The best way to help your students understand this definition is by showing them some examples and nonexamples of polygons, either by drawing examples on the board or using Transparency 0.1, Examples and Non-examples of Polygons.

Line symmetry and *turn symmetry* are illustrated in the introduction to the student edition. You can use Transparency 0.2, Line and Turn Symmetry, to help students better understand these two types of symmetry.

Line symmetry is also called *mirror symmetry* and *folding symmetry.* These terms are helpful for developing students' understanding of this kind of symmetry. A figure has line symmetry if a line can be drawn through the figure so that the part of the figure on one side of the line is reflected exactly onto the part of the figure on the other side of the line. If you have access to mirrors or other reflecting devices, you can use them to help students understand line symmetry.

Turn symmetry is also called *rotational symmetry.* A figure has turn symmetry if it can be rotated around a centerpoint so that it fits exactly onto its original position. You can demonstrate this using Transparency 0.2 and an additional copy of the figure on the right side of the transparency cut from a second piece of transparency film. Place this copy over the figure on the transparency, and stick a pin through the centers of the two figures. Turn the top figure counterclockwise until it again fits over the bottom copy.

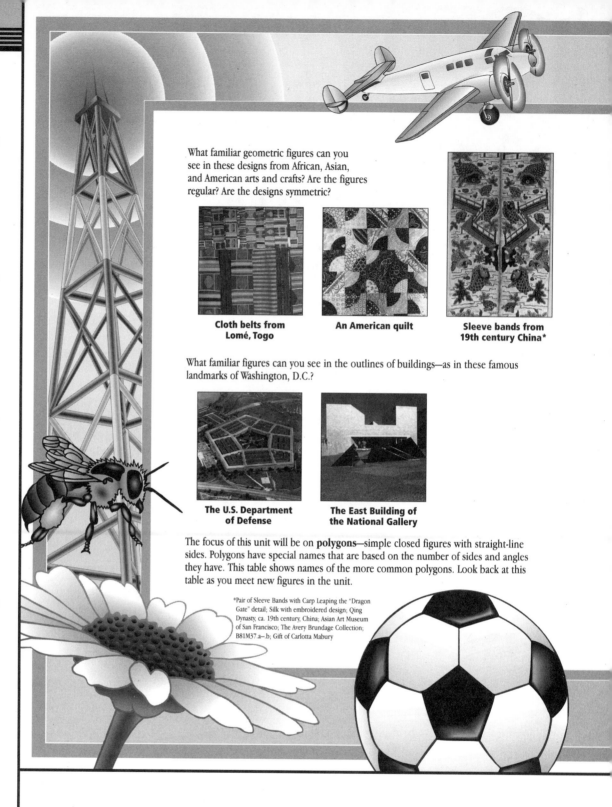

What familiar geometric figures can you see in these designs from African, Asian, and American arts and crafts? Are the figures regular? Are the designs symmetric?

Cloth belts from Lomé, Togo

An American quilt

Sleeve bands from 19th century China*

What familiar figures can you see in the outlines of buildings—as in these famous landmarks of Washington, D.C.?

The U.S. Department of Defense

The East Building of the National Gallery

The focus of this unit will be on **polygons**—simple closed figures with straight-line sides. Polygons have special names that are based on the number of sides and angles they have. This table shows names of the more common polygons. Look back at this table as you meet new figures in the unit.

*Pair of Sleeve Bands with Carp Leaping the "Dragon Gate" detail; Silk with embroidered design; Qing Dynasty, ca. 19th century; China; Asian Art Museum of San Francisco; The Avery Brundage Collection; B81M37.a–.b; Gift of Carlotta Mabury

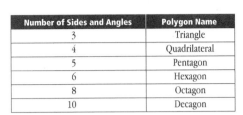

Number of Sides and Angles	Polygon Name
3	Triangle
4	Quadrilateral
5	Pentagon
6	Hexagon
8	Octagon
10	Decagon

As you study the properties of polygons, look for the ways that different combinations of sides and angles give different shapes. In particular, keep your eyes open for shapes that have attractive **symmetries,** such as *line symmetry* and *turn symmetry.* Line symmetry is also called *mirror symmetry,* since the half of the figure on one side of the line looks like it is being reflected in a mirror. Turn symmetry is also called *rotational symmetry,* because you have to rotate the figure around the centerpoint to find the places where it looks the same again.

Line Symmetry	Turn Symmetry
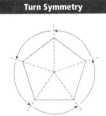	
A polygon with line symmetry has two halves that are mirror images of each other.	A polygon with turn symmetry can be turned around its centerpoint and look the same at certain angles of rotation.

Think about this!

Which common polygons and which kinds of symmetry appear

- in the designs, buildings, and other objects shown on the page before?
- in your classroom, your school, or places outside of your school?

Mathematical Highlights

The Mathematical Highlights page was designed to provide information to students and to parents and other family members. This page gives students a preview of the activities and problems in *Shapes and Designs*. As they work through the unit, students can refer back to the Mathematical Highlights page to review what they have learned and to preview what is still to come. This page also tells parents and other family members what mathematical ideas and activities will be covered as the class works through *Shapes and Designs*.

Mathematical Highlights

In *Shapes and Designs*, you will explore shapes and their properties.

- Using "tiles" in the shapes of polygons leads you to discover which polygons fit together to cover a flat surface. Later, you determine the properties that allow these polygons to fit together so nicely.

- Building triangles and quadrilaterals helps you understand why triangles are used so frequently in bridges, towers, and other structures.

- Honeybee dances, pizza slices, and tree branches are used to illustrate three ways you can think about angles. Measuring angles with an *angle ruler* allows you to find precise angle measurements.

- Using square corners and angles of shapes in your Shapes Set allows you to estimate the measures of many other angles.

- Playing a tic-tac-toe game on a circular grid lets you explore a new kind of coordinate system in which angle measures are used to help locate points.

- Exploring Amelia Earhart's last flight shows you that, in some situations, precise angle measurements are very important.

- Making a table of angle sums for various polygons helps you discover a pattern you can use to determine the angle sum of any polygon.

- Flipping and turning triangles and quadrilaterals demonstrates the angle-side relationships in these figures.

- Writing and debugging computer programs to draw designs and polygons reinforces many of the ideas in this unit.

Using a Calculator

In this unit, you will be able to use your calculator to find patterns in the sums of angle measures in a polygon. You will also be able to determine the sum of the angle measures around the vertex point in a tessellation. As you work on the Connected Mathematics units, you may decide whether using a calculator will help you solve a problem.

Tip for the Linguistically Diverse Classroom

Original Rebus The Original Rebus technique is described in detail in *Getting to Know Connected Mathematics*. Students make their own copy of the text before it is discussed, During discussion, they generate their own rebuses for words they do not understand as the words are made comprehensible through pictures, objects, or demonstrations. Example: Item 2—key words for which students may make rebuses are *triangle, quadrilaterals, bridges, towers, and structures.*

What I Know About Shapes and Designs

As you work in this unit, you will be asked to think about the characteristics of different shapes and how unusual a shape can be and still be a triangle, quadrilateral, pentagon, or hexagon. You will also be asked to think about the relationships among these shapes. It is these characteristics of shapes and the relationships among them that affect the designs you see in your world.

One of the ways you will be asked to demonstrate what sense you are making of the mathematics in this unit is through a final project. At the end of this unit, you will use everything you have learned to create a project, such as a book, a poster, a report, a mobile, a movie, or a slide show.

You can start preparing for your project now. Create a special "shapes section" in your notebook, where you can collect information about:

- The characteristics of the following shapes: triangles, squares, rectangles, parallelograms, quadrilaterals, pentagons, hexagons, octagons
- The relationships among the shapes listed above
- Examples of places where these shapes can be found in your world.

After each investigation, record all the new information you have learned about shapes. Try to use as many of the new vocabulary words as you can. As you work through this unit, keep your eyes open for examples of the shapes listed above being used in many ways. Cut out examples from magazines and newspapers, and draw pictures of shapes you see used in the world around you. You may want to use an envelope for collecting and storing your examples.

At the end of the unit, you should have enough information to make a creative, interesting final project that shows all you have learned about shapes and designs.

Introducing the Unit Project

The final assessment for *Shapes and Designs* is introduced on this page and formally assigned at the end of the unit. Here students are asked to begin collecting drawings, photos, and magazine clippings that show examples of shapes being used in the world around them. Throughout the unit, students are reminded to use the concepts they are learning to write more information about the characteristics of specific shapes. At the end of the unit, students are asked to create projects that show all they have learned about shapes and designs.

It is recommended that you introduce the project prior to Investigation 1. Students could start a special "shapes section" in their notebook to record what they are learning about shapes. Students should add to their "shapes section" throughout the unit. Remind students to use their vocabulary words as they write about the different shapes. A periodic sharing of examples during class may also help encourage students to see shapes around them. Encourage them to add to their own entries after hearing the ideas of others.

See page 76 for information about assigning the project. For a possible scoring rubric and samples of student projects, see page 96.

The Investigations

The teaching materials for each investigation consist of three parts: an overview, the student pages with teaching outlines, and the detailed notes for teaching the investigation.

The overview of each investigation includes brief descriptions of the problems, the mathematical and problem-solving goals of the investigation, and a list of necessary materials.

Essential information for teaching the investigation is provided in the margins around the student pages. The "At a Glance" overviews are brief outlines of the Launch, Explore, and Summarize phases of each problem for reference as you work with the class. To help you assign homework, a list of "Assignment Choices" is provided next to each problem. Wherever space permits, answers to problems, follow-ups, ACE questions, and Mathematical Reflections appear next to the appropriate student pages.

The Teaching the Investigation section follows the student pages and is the heart of the Connected Mathematics curriculum. This section describes in detail the Launch, Explore, and Summarize phases for each problem. It includes all the information needed for teaching, along with suggestions for what you might say at key points in the teaching. Use this section to prepare lessons and as a guide for teaching an investigation.

Assessment Resources

The Assessment Resources section contains blackline masters and answer keys for the quiz, check-ups, and the Question Bank. It also provides guidelines for assessing the Unit Project and other important student work. Samples of student work, along with the teacher's comments about how each sample was assessed, will help you to evaluate your students' efforts. Blackline masters for the Notebook Checklist and the Self-Assessment are given. These instruments support student self-evaluation, an important aspect of assessment in the Connected Mathematics curriculum.

Blackline Masters

The Blackline Masters section includes masters for all labsheets and transparencies. Blackline masters of grid paper, isometric dot paper, the ShapeSet, and Polystrips are also provided.

Additional Practice

Practice pages for each investigation offer additional problems for students who need more practice with the basic concepts developed in the investigations as well as some continual review of earlier concepts.

Descriptive Glossary

The Descriptive Glossary provides descriptions and examples of the key concepts in *Shapes and Designs*. These descriptions are not intended to be formal definitions, but are meant to give you an idea of how students might make sense of these important concepts.

Bees and Polygons

Many students are interested in bees and beehives. This topic recurs throughout this unit and comes up again in the *Covering and Surrounding* unit. In this unit, we explore the shape seen on the face of honeycombs and the ways bees communicate with each other about the location of nectar for their honey production.

This short investigation poses the question, How do the shapes of figures determine whether they can tile a plane? In Problem 1.1, Tiling a Beehive, students talk about what makes a polygon a regular polygon, and investigate which regular polygons and combinations of regular polygons can be used to tile a surface. The questions posed in Problem 1.1 and the ACE section will pique students' curiosity and provide a common reference for future investigations.

Mathematical and Problem-Solving Goals

- **To discover, through exploration, which regular polygons can be used to tile a plane**

- **To discover combinations of regular polygons that can be used to tile a plane**

- **To discover that some irregular polygons can be used to tile a plane**

Materials		
Problem	**For students**	**For the teacher**
All	Calculators, ShapesSet (1 per group)	Transparency 1.1, ShapeSet for use on overhead projector (optional; copy the blackline masters onto transparency film)
ACE	ShapeSet	

Tiling a Beehive

At a Glance

Grouping:
Small Groups

Launch

- Discuss the material about bees from the student edition, focusing on the shapes—hexagons—that cover the face of a honeycomb.

- Discuss the definition of *regular polygon* and show examples to help clarify.

Explore

- Circulate while students work in groups to find which regular polygons and combinations of regular polygons can be used to tile a surface.

- Encourage students to record and make sketches of their results.

Summarize

- Hold a class discussion in which students share their results with the class.

Bees and Polygons

Honeybees live in colonies. In the wild, bee colonies build nests. Beekeepers provide wooden boxes called *hives* for the colonies they keep. About 60,000 residents are packed into a hive. Bees are fairly small insects, but packing a hive with 60,000 bees and their honey is tricky. Bees store their honey in a honeycomb, which is filled with tubes. An interesting pattern of polygons appears on the face of a honeycomb: it is covered with a design of identical hexagons that fit together like tiles on a floor.

Why do you think honeycombs are covered with hexagons instead of some other shape?

Did you know?

Each honeybee colony has a single queen and thousands of female *worker bees*. The worker bees find flowers to get nectar for making honey. They build the honeycomb, keep the beehive clean, take care of baby bees, feed and groom the queen bee, and guard the hive against intruders. Every hive also has several male bees, called *drones*, who have only one job: to fly around looking for a queen from another colony to mate with. Once a drone bee has mated, it dies.

Assignment Choices

ACE questions 1–8, 12, and 13

Tip for the Linguistically Diverse Classroom

Rebus Scenario The Rebus Scenario technique is described in detail in *Getting to Know Connected Mathematics*. This technique involves sketching rebuses on the chalkboard that correspond to key words in the story or information you present orally. Example: some key words for which you may need to draw rebuses while discussing the Did You Know? feature—*queen bee* (a bee with a crown), *flower* (a simple flower), *honeycomb* (several hexagons joined together), and *guard* (bee with soldier attire in front of hive).

1.1 Tiling a Beehive

The shapes pictured below are examples of **regular polygons**. The word *regular* means that all sides and angles of the polygon are the same size. (The *edges* of a figure are sometimes called the *sides* of a figure. Both words are correct.)

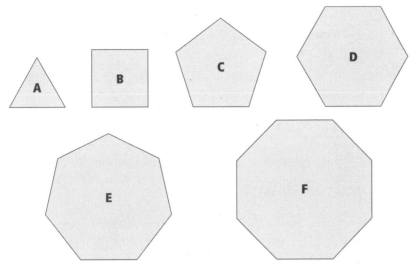

The honeycomb demonstrates that regular hexagons fit together to cover, or *tile*, a surface. Are there other shapes that have this same property?

Problem 1.1

Tiling means covering a flat surface with shapes that fit together without any gaps. Which of the regular polygons shown above will tile a flat surface?

Use shapes A–F from your ShapeSet or cutouts of the shapes shown above to explore this question. As you work, try to figure out why some shapes cover a space, while others do not. Consider two types of tilings:

A. Patterns in which all the tiles are the same

B. Patterns that combine two or more different tiles

As you experiment, make sketches to share with your classmates. Keep a record of shapes and combinations of shapes that cover a surface and those that do not.

Answers to Problem 1.1

A. Squares, triangles, and hexagons can be used alone to cover a surface. Later, students will discover that this is because the angle measures of these shapes are factors of 360. The pentagon, heptagon, and octagon will not tile a surface (because their angle measures are not factors of 360).

B. Examples of combinations that work are octagons and squares, hexagons and triangles, and squares and triangles.

Problem 1.1 Follow-Up

Look back at each tiling you made. Find a point on the tiling where the corners of the polygons fit together. This point is called a *vertex* of the tiling. For each tiling, describe exactly which polygons fit around a vertex and in what order they fit together.

> **Did you know?**
>
> Tilings are also called *tessellations*. Artists, designers, and mathematicians have been interested in tessellations for centuries. The Greek mathematician and inventor Archimedes (c. 287–212 B.C.) studied the properties of regular polygons that tiled the plane. From 700–1500 B.C., Moorish artists—forbidden by their religion to paint people, animals, and other real-world objects—used tessellating patterns extensively in their work. The Dutch artist M. C. Escher (1898–1972), inspired by Moorish designs, spent his life creating tessellations. He altered geometric tessellating shapes to make birds, reptiles, fish, and people.

Answer to Problem 1.1 Follow-Up

Possible answer: Six triangles, four squares, or three hexagons fit around a point. Two octagons and one square fit around a point. Two hexagons and four triangles fit around a point in the following order: hexagon, triangle, triangle, hexagon, triangle, triangle. Two squares and three triangles will fit together in the following order: triangle, triangle, triangle, square, square.

As you work on these ACE questions, use your calculator whenever you need it.

Applications

1. Choose a rectangle from your ShapeSet, or draw your own. Find several ways that copies of your rectangle can be used to cover, or tile, a surface. Make sketches of the patterns you discover.

2. The shapes shown below are *parallelograms*. Choose a parallelogram from your ShapeSet or draw your own. Find several ways that copies of your parallelogram can be used to cover, or tile, a surface. Make sketches of the patterns you discover.

3. Choose a triangle from your ShapeSet, or draw your own. Find several ways that copies of your triangle can be used to cover, or tile, a surface. Make sketches of the patterns you discover.

Connections

4. Name the polygon that appears in each of these street signs. If you need help, refer to the table of polygon names on page 5.

Answers

Applications

1. Answers will vary. Many interesting patterns can be made from a rectangle.

2. Answers will vary. Look at how the students' shapes fit together. There should be no overlap, and it should be clear how parallelograms could continue to be added at the sides to extend the tiling indefinitely.

3. See page 14c.

Connections

4. East Lansing: rectangle; Stop: octagon; School Zone: pentagon; Construction: square or rhombus; Yield: triangle

5. 1 row of 30, 2 rows of 15, 3 rows of 10, 5 rows of 6, and their opposites (such as 30 rows of 1)

6. 1 row of 24, 2 rows of 12, 3 rows of 8, 4 rows of 6, and their opposites

7. 1 row of 36, 2 rows of 18, 3 rows of 12, 6 rows of 6, and their opposites

8. 1 row of 17 and its opposite

Extensions

9. Answers will vary.

(Teaching Tip: If you or your students are particularly interested in flags, you could make a display of flags that focuses on the shapes that flags contain. Some students may want to make their own flags or research the symbolism of the various colors and shapes.)

10. See below right.

In 5–8, find the dimensions of all the possible rectangles that can be made with the given number of square tiles. For example, the rectangle at right is made with 2 rows of 3 tiles each. We say that the *dimensions* of this rectangle are 2×3.

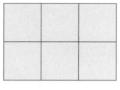

5. 30 square tiles   **6.** 24 square tiles

7. 36 square tiles   **8.** 17 square tiles

Extensions

9. Find pictures of American state flags and flags of other countries in a dictionary or encyclopedia. Sketch several flags that you think show interesting uses of geometric shapes in their design. Explain what you find interesting about the flags. Then draw a design that you would use as a flag of your own.

State flag of Maryland

In 10 and 11, create tiling patterns that use copies of both of the shapes in each pair. Use these shapes from your Shapes Set or cutouts of the shapes to help you find patterns. Make sketches of the patterns you discover.

10.

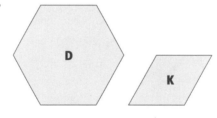

---

10. The sides of the pieces must match up and the angles must be correct for these to work. Since the hexagon can be cut into three of the parallelograms (as illustrated), this could be made into a tiling of parallelograms. Here is one possible tiling:

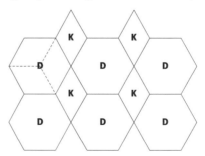

11.

12. Below is a large square tiled with identical, smaller squares. Which other regular polygons can be tiled with identical, smaller copies of themselves? Sketch any patterns you think will work.

13. An *irregular polygon*, such as the one shown below, is a polygon in which the sides are not all the same length. Choose an irregular quadrilateral from your Shapes Set, or draw your own. Cut out several copies of your figure and see whether you can use them to tile a surface. Sketch your findings. Test other irregular quadrilaterals to see if they can be used to tile a surface. Summarize what you find about using quadrilaterals to tile a surface.

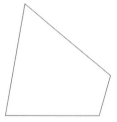

14. Can you make a tiling pattern with circles? Why or why not?

15. Does a circle have any turn symmetries? If so, explain and show some examples.

11. See below left.

12. See page 14c.

13. See page 14d.

14. Circles by themselves will not tile a surface, as they do not fit together without overlaps or gaps. To tile with a circle, you would need another tile in the shape of the gap that is created between the circles. This piece, of course, would not be a polygon.

15. The circle is very rich in line and turn symmetries. Any line through the center of the circle (a diameter) is a mirror line. Any amount of turn around the centerpoint of the figure will make the figure fit into exactly the same position.

11. The angles and sides of this trapezoid and parallelogram are compatible, so they will tile a plane. The following is one way to put the pieces together. You can see that this tiling can also be viewed as a tiling of hexagons with some new edges drawn.

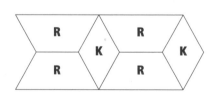

1. From among the regular polygons, only triangles, squares, and hexagons will tile the plane when used alone. For equilateral triangles, it takes six figures to surround a vertex point. For squares, it takes four figures to surround a vertex point. For hexagons, it takes three figures.

2. Several combinations of regular shapes will tile the plane. Here are some that students may find (the figures surround each vertex point in the order given):

- three triangles and two squares

- a hexagon, a square, a triangle, and a square

- two octagons and a square

- four triangles and a hexagon

- a square, a triangle, a square, and two triangles

- a hexagon, a triangle, a hexagon, and a triangle

- a square, a hexagon, and a dodecagon

- a triangle and two dodecagons

The eight combinations above, plus the three regular polygons that can tile a surface alone, are the only tilings possible from regular polygons if the arrangement of polygons at every vertex point is identical. The eight tilings made from combined regular polygons are called *semiregular tessellations*.

Mathematical Reflections

In this investigation, you found that some shapes can tile a surface, while others cannot. These questions will help you summarize what you have learned:

1 Which shapes seem to work as tiles and which do not?

2 Which polygons can tile alone and which need to be combined with other polygons to fill a space?

Think about your answers to these questions, discuss your ideas with other students and your teacher, and then write a summary of your findings in your journal.

Are you keeping your eyes open? What shapes and designs are you noticing in the world around you? Remember to write what you have discovered about triangles, squares, rectangles, parallelograms, quadrilaterals, pentagons, hexagons, and octagons from this investigation.

Tip for the Linguistically Diverse Classroom

Diagram Code The Diagram Code technique is described in detail in *Getting to Know Connected Mathematics*. Students use a minimal number of words with drawings or diagrams to respond to questions that require writing. Example: Question 2—A student might answer this question by drawing a picture of a hexagon, a square, and a triangle with the words *Yes/Alone* underneath and another picture of an octagon and a square with the words *Yes/Combined*.

TEACHING THE INVESTIGATION

1.1 • Tiling a Beehive

In *Shapes and Designs*, students explore hexagons and other shapes that can be used to cover a surface and discover some of the properties of these shapes that allow them to fit together so nicely. In the *Covering and Surrounding* unit, students will investigate why, of all the shapes that can tile a surface, honeycombs might be covered with hexagons. In this problem, students explore what other shapes might work to cover a surface.

Launch

Read the material about honeybees on page 8 aloud to the class. The "Did You Know?" discussion of honeybees and their habits will probably elicit many comments from students about their own encounters with and ideas about bees. You will want to focus the discussion on the shapes—regular hexagons—that cover the face of a honeycomb.

> Suppose you were a creative honeybee and you wanted to build a different kind of honeycomb. What shapes besides hexagons might you use?

This leads the discussion into Problem 1.1. Discuss the definition of *regular polygon,* and help students to see that the polygons shown fit this definition by measuring the sides (or checking them visually) and by pointing out that the angles look similar. This is not the time to use a protractor or angle ruler. It is, however, a good time to find out whether students understand the terms *side* and *angle,* and what it means for two sides or two angles to be the same size. Informal information is enough at this time, since these ideas are thoroughly developed in Investigation 3.

Explore

Students could work in pairs or groups of three on Problem 1.1. Give them time to talk about and experiment with the shapes. Their answers should be visual representations of their discoveries, about which they might write concluding statements.

One issue students are likely to bring up is whether a tiling has to fit exactly inside the sides of the space being filled. For example, a rectangular patio may be constructed with hexagonal tiles, but the tiles at the side of the patio would have to be portions of complete hexagons. Explain that the usual condition is that although the space is to be completely filled, we can cut off shapes that extend over its side. The hexagons on a honeycomb don't fit exactly into a square or rectangular frame; some shapes near the side must be partial hexagons.

Students should go beyond showing six triangles tiling, four pentagons not tiling, and so on. Encourage them to explore patterns made with a single kind of tile and patterns made with combinations of tiles. You will probably need to remind them to record their results for shapes that don't tile a surface, as well as for combinations of shapes that do.

Summarize

When all groups have found shapes and combinations of shapes that work and don't work, have them share their results by drawing them on the board or showing them on the overhead projector. To help your students notice which individual shapes create a tiling and which combinations of shapes do, you can create a chart on the board to keep track of each new finding. The chart could have two columns labeled "Individual Shapes that Tile" and "Combinations of Shapes that Tile."

Here are some things students have discovered:

DJ said he could tile the paper with the square. He showed this pattern on the overhead:

Adell said she could tile the paper with the triangle. She showed the class this pattern:

Faaiz said he could tile the paper with the triangle and the square. He put together this pattern on the overhead:

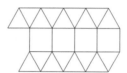

When students have had time to determine which polygons would tile a honeycomb and have presented their findings to the class, you might again initiate the question, Why hexagons? Students should have eliminated all but the triangle, square, and hexagon as possibilities for tiling, but may not yet have ruled out the triangle and square as candidates for the tiling of a honeycomb. That is an acceptable place to leave the conjecture at this time.

For the Teacher: Using Shorthand Notation

Some teachers use this opportunity to explain a shorthand notation for describing the regular polygons and combinations of regular polygons used in the tiling patterns. In this notation, DJ's tiling of squares is written 4, 4, 4, 4. The numerals indicate the number of sides the regular polygons have; the 4s indicate squares. Four 4s indicate that four squares surround each vertex point in the pattern. Adell's triangle tiling would be written 3, 3, 3, 3, 3, 3, since each triangle has three sides and six triangles surround each vertex point. Faaiz's tiling of triangles and squares could be written 4, 3, 3, 3, 4, indicating that two squares (the 4s) and three triangles (the 3s) surround each vertex point. The order of the numbers indicates that, as you proceed clockwise around a vertex point, the shapes follow the pattern square, triangle, triangle, triangle, square.

Additional Answers

ACE Answers

Applications

3. Answers will vary. All triangles will tile a flat surface.

For the Teacher: Extending ACE Question 3

There is very interesting mathematics in question 3. The fact that all triangles have 180° as the sum of their angles means that two copies of each angle of a triangle will surround a vertex point. To make the tiling grow, you have to make sure that sides of the same length are put together. The following diagram, with angles labeled, shows a general pattern that will work for any triangle. You can discuss these ideas with students who are ready to think harder about tiling with triangles.

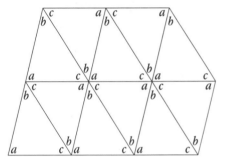

Extensions

12. The equilateral triangle is the only other regular polygon that can be tiled in this way. You can see this by connecting the midpoints of each side of an equilateral triangle to form an upside-down triangle in the center. This subdivides the triangle into four smaller triangles that are the same shape as the original. This technique works for *any* triangle! Here is an irregular triangle cut into smaller, identical triangles:

Martin Gardner calls all shapes that can be tiled in this way—including the parallelogram,

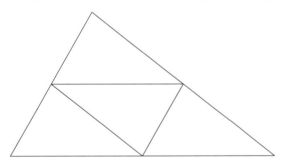

certain trapezoids, and some other strange shapes—*reptiles* (repeating tiles). There is an entire activity on reptiles in the *Middle Grades Mathematics Project* unit on similarity.[1] This topic is covered in the *Stretching and Shrinking* unit, so don't feel it is necessary to cover it here.

[1] Lappan, Glenda, et. al., *Similarity and Equivalent Fractions* (Menlo Park: Addison-Wesley, 1986).

13. An irregular quadrilateral will tile a surface. Because there is a total of 360° in the angles of a quadrilateral, one of each angle must surround each vertex point in the pattern. As with a triangle, sides that are the same length must be put together. A way to help students see the pattern and to see that the pattern works for any quadrilateral is to label the sides. This shows that there are copies of each of the angles of the quadrilateral around each vertex point, and that the sides are always placed so that the lengths match and the labels are reversed.

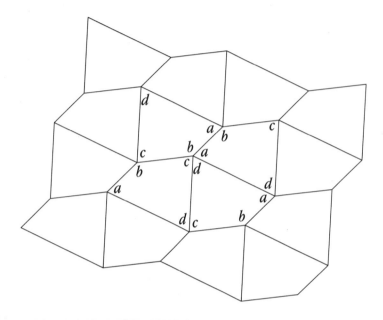

For the Teacher: Tiling with an Irregular Quadrilateral

It will not be easy for students to see how to tile using the irregular quadrilateral. If no one discovers how to do a tiling with that shape (or for that matter, any one of the other shapes they are exploring), we recommend that you leave it as an open question for students to work on (rather than showing them yourself).

Building Polygons

In this investigation, students explore the ways that side lengths determine the shape of polygons. In each of the three problems, students try to construct polygons with various combinations of side lengths.

Students move from experimenting with three-sided polygons in Problem 2.1, Building Triangles, to working with four-sided polygons in Problem 2.2, Building Quadrilaterals, and Problem 2.3, Building Parallelograms. In their experimentation, they discover properties of polygons that will help them to understand an important principle and the dominant theme of this investigation: side lengths determine the exact shape of a triangle (as long as the sum of the lengths of any pair of sides is longer than the length of the third side), but for other polygons, in general, side lengths can be arranged in a variety of shapes. This principle underlies the use of triangles in construction bracing. The triangle is a stable figure, whereas quadrilaterals, for instance, can wobble into many unstable shapes. This property of triangles is expressed in formal geometry as the *Side-Side-Side Congruence Theorem*.

Mathematical and Problem-Solving Goals

- **To understand that triangles are stable figures that keep their shape under stress**

- **To discover the triangle inequality— the sum of the lengths of any two sides of a triangle is greater than the length of the third side—through experimentation**

- **To discover that quadrilaterals and other polygons are not stable shapes and become distorted under stress**

- **To discover that the sum of the lengths of any three sides of a quadrilateral is greater than the length of the fourth side**

Materials		
Problem	For students	For the teacher
All	Calculators, polystrips, brass fasteners	Transparencies 2.1 to 2.3 (optional), polystrips, brass fasteners
2.1	Large sheets of unlined paper for groups to record answers, number cubes (3 per group, optional)	
2.2	Large sheets of unlined paper for groups to record answers, number cubes (3 per group, optional), isometric dot paper (provided as a blackline master)	
2.3		A few quadrilaterals cut out of paper, including parallelograms, rectangles, and squares (to supplement those students create for the Launch of Problem 2.3)

Student Pages 15–21   Teaching the Investigation 21a–21g

INVESTIGATION 2

Building Polygons

Polygons come in many shapes and sizes. You can use polystrips and fasteners like these:

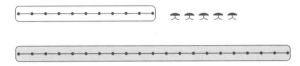

to build polygons and study their properties.

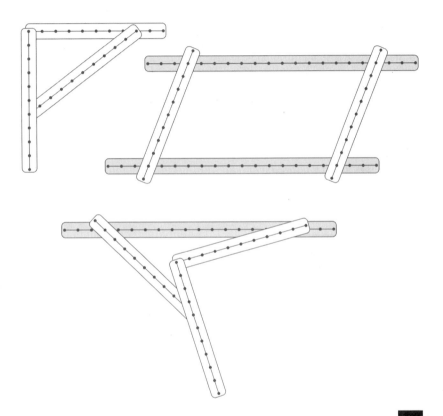

Investigation 2: Building Polygons **15**

Answers to Problem 2.1

A. no; Not every combination of three sides will make a triangle. To make a triangle, the sum of the lengths of any two sides must be greater than the length of the third side.

B. no; There is only one triangle possible from three side lengths. (This is what gives triangles the stability that makes them useful in buildings and other structures.)

Building Triangles

At a Glance

Grouping:
Small Groups

Launch

- Discuss the question of whether any three side lengths will make a triangle.

- Demonstrate how to use Polystrips to make triangles and how to keep a record of findings.

Explore

- Circulate while students work in groups to explore whether any three numbers can serve as side lengths for a triangle.

- Encourage students to record and make sketches of their results.

Summarize

- Hold a class discussion in which students share and compare their results.

Triangles are the simplest polygons. Although they have only three sides and three angles, triangles come in many different shapes with very useful properties. You can use polystrips to experiment with building triangles and to discover some important properties and characteristics about them. Problem 2.1 asks you to explore questions about the side lengths of triangles: If you are given three side lengths, can you always make a triangle? With three side lengths, can you make more than one triangle?

Problem 2.1

Suppose you are given three numbers to be lengths of sides in a triangle.

A. Will it always be possible to make a triangle with those side lengths?

B. Can you make two or more different triangles from the same side lengths?

Explore these questions by first selecting three numbers between 1 and 20 and then using polystrips to try to make a triangle with the numbers as side lengths. Repeat this several times with many different sets of three numbers. Sketch and label your results so you can share them with the class.

A good way to select numbers is to use number cubes. Toss three cubes, and use their sum as the length of one side. Toss the cubes two more times to get lengths for the other two sides.

■ Problem 2.1 Follow-Up

When you have completed the problem, look back over your examples, and use polystrips to explore these questions.

1. What combinations of side lengths give triangles like those you see often in designs and buildings?
2. What combinations of side lengths give triangles with strange shapes?
3. What combinations of side lengths give triangles that have symmetry?

When you make an interesting triangle, trace it on a large sheet of paper so you can share it with the class. On the paper, explain why you think the triangle is interesting. Be sure to focus on the *mathematical* properties that make the shape interesting.

Assignment Choices

ACE questions 1, 2, 5, and 7, and unassigned choices from earlier problems

Answers to Problem 2.1

See page 15

Answers to Problem 2.1 Follow-Up

1. Possible answers: three sides that are the same length; two sides that are the same length.

2. Possible answers: one long edge and two short edges; three sides that are very different lengths.

3. Possible answers: triangles that look more regular; triangles with all three sides equal; triangles with two sides equal.

2.2 Building Quadrilaterals

A polygon with four sides is called a **quadrilateral.** Many different kinds of quadrilaterals appear in the structures and designs all around us. In the last problem, you explored triangles and discovered some important properties about them. In this problem, you will explore quadrilaterals. As you work with quadrilaterals, think about ways quadrilaterals and triangles are similar and ways they are different.

Problem 2.2

Suppose you are given four numbers to be lengths of sides in a quadrilateral.

A. Will it always be possible to make a quadrilateral with those side lengths?

B. Can you make two or more different quadrilaterals from the same side lengths?

Explore these questions by first selecting four numbers between 1 and 20 and then using polystrips to try to make a quadrilateral with the numbers as side lengths. Repeat this several times with many different sets of four numbers. Sketch and label your results so you can share them with the class.

A good way to select numbers is to use number cubes. Toss three cubes, and use their sum as the length of one side. Toss the cubes three more times to get lengths for the other three sides.

■ Problem 2.2 Follow-Up

When you have completed the problem, look back over your examples, and use polystrips to explore these questions.

1. What combinations of side lengths give quadrilaterals like those you see often in designs and buildings?
2. What combinations of side lengths give quadrilaterals with strange shapes?
3. What combinations of side lengths give quadrilaterals that have symmetry?

When you make an interesting quadrilateral, trace it on a large sheet of paper so you can share it with the class. On the paper, explain why you think the quadrilateral is interesting. Be sure to focus on the *mathematical* properties that make the shape interesting.

Building Quadrilaterals

At a Glance

**Grouping:
Small Groups**

Launch

- Pose the question of whether any four side lengths will make a quadrilateral and whether four side lengths will make a *unique* quadrilateral.
- Discuss the issue of how to keep a record of findings.

Explore

- Circulate while students work in groups to explore whether any four numbers can serve as side lengths for a quadrilateral and whether four side lengths determine a unique quadrilateral.

Summarize

- Hold a class discussion in which students compare their results.
- Discuss ways of forming different quadrilaterals from a given set of side lengths.
- Explore the quadrilaterals that result from various combinations of side lengths.

Answers to Problem 2.2

A. no; No side can be equal to or greater in length than the sum of the lengths of the other three sides.

B. yes; Many (actually, an infinite number of) different quadrilaterals can be made with the same set of sides by changing the order of the sides or positioning the angles differently (shearing or "squishing" the quadrilateral).

Answers to Problem 2.2 Follow-Up

See page 21g.

Assignment Choices

ACE questions 3, 4, 6, 8, 10, 14, and unassigned choices from earlier problems

Have students make quadrilaterals from isometric dot paper (see "Summarize" on page 21d)

2.3

Building Parallelograms

At a Glance

**Grouping:
Small Groups**

Launch

- In a class activity, have students sort the quadrilaterals they made at home into parallelograms and nonparallelograms.

- Discuss some of the special properties of rectangles and squares as subsets within the set of parallelograms.

Explore

- Circulate while students work in groups to explore the relationships between rectangles and parallelograms.

- Encourage students to articulate what characteristics a parallelogram must have.

Summarize

- As a class, develop a list of characteristics of parallelograms.

2.3 Building Parallelograms

Rectangles may be the most common quadrilaterals. You can find them in buildings and designs everywhere. Here are five examples of rectangles:

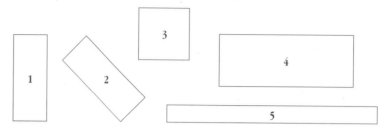

In your work with polystrips, you probably discovered that if you build a rectangle and then push on one of its corners, it easily changes into different shapes, such as these:

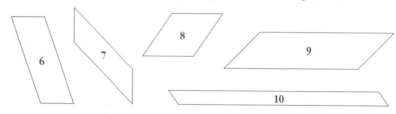

Problem 2.3

The ten quadrilaterals shown above are examples of **parallelograms**. The name *parallelogram* is based on the word *parallel*. Parallel lines are straight lines that never meet, no matter how far they are extended.

A. What do these ten quadrilaterals have in common that makes the name *parallelogram* sensible?

B. How do rectangles 1–5 differ from shapes 6–10 (which were formed by pressing on the corners of 1–5)?

C. How are the lengths of the sides of a parallelogram related?

Explore these questions by making a variety of parallelograms with polystrips. Sketch the results so you can share them with the class.

■ **Problem 2.3 Follow-Up**

Describe what happens to the four angles in the rectangle as you slowly push on a corner of the polystrip model.

Assignment Choices

Unassigned choices from previous problems

Answers to Problem 2.3

A. Their opposite sides are parallel.

B. Rectangles 1–5 all have only right angles.

C. Both pairs of opposite sides are equal in length.

Answer to Problem 2.3 Follow-Up

Possible answer: As you press on the corner of a Polystrip rectangle, the angle at that corner gets larger and the angle at an adjacent corner gets smaller. As the shape of the quadrilateral changes, opposite angles are always equal.

As you work on these ACE questions, use your calculator whenever you need it.

Applications

In 1–8, sketch examples of shapes that can be made with the given set of side lengths. Be prepared to explain your strategy for finding examples and to discuss whether your examples are all that are possible.

1. Side lengths of 5, 5, and 3

2. Side lengths of 8, 8, and 8

3. Side lengths of 5, 5, 8, and 8

4. Side lengths of 5, 5, 6, and 14

5. Side lengths of 5, 8, and 15

6. Side lengths of 8, 8, 8, and 8

7. Side lengths of 5, 6, and 10

8. Side lengths of 4, 3, 5, and 14

In 9–12, determine which set or sets of side lengths from 1–8 above can make the following shapes.

9. A triangle with all angles the same size

10. A quadrilateral with all angles the same size

11. A parallelogram

12. A quadrilateral that is not a parallelogram

Connections

13. a. In what ways are all three quadrilaterals below alike?

   b. In what ways does each quadrilateral differ from the others?

3.   These sides will make parallelograms or kites (figures with two pairs of adjacent, congruent sides), depending on whether the two same-length sides are side by side or separated.

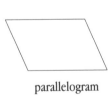

parallelogram

kite

Answers

Applications

1.   The only possibility is a 5–5–3 isosceles triangle.

2.   The only possibility is an 8–8–8 equilateral triangle.

3.   See below left.

4.   These sides will make quadrilaterals with sides with order 5–5–6–14 or 5–6–5–14.

5.   No triangle can be made with these side lengths. 15 is greater than 5 + 8.

6.   These sides will make rhombuses (including the special rhombus with right angles, the square).

7.   The only possibility is a 5–6–10 triangle.

8.   No polygon can be made with these side lengths. The side of 14 units is greater than the sum of the other three sides.

9.   If all angles are equal, all sides must also be equal. The 8–8–8 triangle in question 2 is the only possibility.

10.   A quadrilateral with all angles equal must be a rectangle. The side lengths in question 3 can be connected in 5–8–5–8 order to form a rectangle. The side lengths in question 6 can form a square (a special rectangle).

11.   A parallelogram must have two pairs of opposite equal sides. The side lengths in question 3 can be connected in 5–8–5–8 order to form a parallelogram. The side lengths in question 6 can form a rhombus (a special parallelogram).

12. The side lengths in question 3 can be arranged in 5–5–8–8 order to form a kite. The side lengths in questions 4 and 8 will always form quadrilaterals that are not parallelograms.

Connections

13a. All three have four sides and four angles. The opposite sides are equal in each.

13b. In the square, all sides are equal. In the rectangle, adjacent sides are not equal, but all angles are 90°. Figure 3 does not have any right angles.

14. Triangles are stable shapes, so they help a structure to keep its shape.

Extensions

15a. Possible answer: Designs incorporating pentagons are probably easier to make and more common when all the sides are the same length.

15b. no; No side can be longer than the sum of the other four sides.

15c. yes; All you need to do is change the order of the sides and you have a new pentagon. Also, any pentagon can be "squished" into other pentagons.

16a. This is not a closed form.

16b. The sides are curved.

16c. The sides overlap.

17. See right.

---

14. Based on your polystrip work with triangles and quadrilaterals, what explanations can you now give for the common appearance of triangular shapes in figures like radio and TV towers and in bridges?

Extensions

15. A polygon with five sides is called a **pentagon**. In a–c, explore some pentagon shapes by using polystrips or making sketches.

a. What combinations of side lengths give pentagons that you think are especially good for use in designs?

b. Is it always possible to make a pentagon with any given five numbers as side lengths? Explain.

c. Can you make two or more different pentagons from the same side lengths? Explain.

16. The shapes below are *not* polygons, although they are similar to polygons in some ways. In a–c, explain how the shape is different from the polygons pictured earlier in this unit.

a.   **b.**   **c.**

17. What symmetries do each of the figures in question 16 have? Show and explain your answers.

17a. This figure has no line symmetry, but it has 180° turn symmetry around the midpoint of the middle step.

17b. This figure has line symmetry over the line drawn from the peak to the middle of the base. It has only the trivial 360° turn symmetry.

17c. This figure has only the trivial 360° turn symmetry.

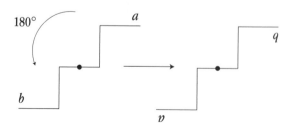

Mathematical Reflections

In this investigation, you experimented with building polygons by choosing lengths for the sides, and then connecting those sides to make a simple closed figure. These questions will help you summarize what you have learned:

1. How many different triangles can you make from a set of three side lengths?

2. How can you tell by looking at the lengths of three line segments whether they can be used to form a triangle?

3. How many different quadrilaterals can you make from a set of four side lengths?

4. What combinations of side lengths will always give a parallelogram? A rectangle? A square?

Think about your answers to these questions, discuss your ideas with other students and your teacher, and then write a summary of your findings in your journal.

Remember to collect pictures and make drawings of how the shapes you are learning about are used in the world around you! In the project section of your journal, record what you have discovered about triangles and quadrilaterals.

Tip for the Linguistically Diverse Classroom

Diagram Code The Diagram Code technique is described in detail in *Getting to Know Connected Mathematics*. Students use a minimal number of words with drawings or diagrams to respond to questions that require writing. Example: Question 1—A student might answer this question by drawing the same triangle (perhaps with labeled sides) in seveeral positions with the words *1 Triangle* underneath.

Possible Answers

1. The unique thing about triangles compared to other polygons is that side lengths completely determine a triangle. Even though we can turn or flip a triangle into different-looking positions, only one triangle shape can be made from a given set of side lengths.

2. The sum of any two sides must be longer than the remaining side. Some students may give the equally correct version: the lengths of the two shorter sides must add to more than the length of the longest side.

3. You can make an infinite number, since the quadrilateral is not a stable shape and can be made into different quadrilaterals by changing the angles. You can also put the four side lengths in different orders to make different quadrilaterals.

4. A parallelogram will always result from sides that fit the pattern *a, b, a, b*, meaning that opposite side lengths must be equal. A rectangle requires the same conditions on lengths and arrangement of sides, but its angles must be fixed at 90°. A square requires all lengths to be equal and all angles to be fixed at 90°.

TEACHING THE INVESTIGATION

2.1 • Building Triangles

This problem is a student experiment with a manipulative called *Polystrips*. Students begin by considering the question of whether *any* three lengths will make a triangle. Students are to choose three numbers, each 20 or less, and then try to construct a triangle from those side lengths. They keep a record of their work and return to their data to look for common and unusual triangles and triangles with symmetry. Keeping track of their discoveries is a critical skill for students to develop.

Launch

Help students to be conscientious when using the Polystrips to represent the length they want. It is the space *between* two holes that represents a length of one unit. We count spaces, not holes. (It's the fence-post problem. It takes three fence posts to hold up two lengths of fence. If we want to know how long the fence is, we count fence sections, not posts.) You may want to number the holes (starting with zero) on the Polystrips so students can immediately find the given length.

It is a good idea to demonstrate how to use the Polystrips and count side lengths. First, choose three numbers under 20, and build a triangle with the Polystrips using those numbers as side lengths. Then, have each group build a 6–8–12 triangle, and check to see that each group knows how to fasten the strips together to represent the lengths. When the students understand how to manipulate the Polystrips, raise the question of the relationship among the lengths of the sides of a triangle.

> Do you think we can make a triangle using any three lengths for the sides?

Let a student or two give an opinion.

> We are going to conduct an experiment to gather some data to help us with this question. We want to look for relationships that will let us predict—without building—whether three given line segments will make a triangle. Let's record the example we did together as our first piece of data.

Record the following on the board.

Side 1	Side 2	Side 3	Makes a Triangle?
6	8	12	Yes

> In your groups, you will choose three numbers to be the lengths of the sides of a triangle. Use Polystrips to test the three lengths. Record exactly what your numbers are and whether or not they will make a triangle. Then, repeat the test with three new numbers. As you select lengths for the sides, try to create interesting and different triangles.

Explain to students that keeping an accurate record of their data is very important because it allows them to recreate examples as evidence of what they discovered.

Explore

Allow students to work in groups of two or three on the problem. Let students either make up sets of numbers—all less than 20—or roll three number cubes and use the sum of the faces as the length of a side. Rolling number cubes is an easy way to generate an interesting variety of lengths and is particularly useful for a group that is having trouble making up numbers to try.

Make sure students keep the question of whether any three lengths will make a triangle at the center of their group discussions. In addition, they need to focus on the question of whether three side lengths give a unique triangle or allow different triangles to be made. A key question is, What is meant by the word *different* when we are referring to shape, as in *different shape?* The standard test for determining whether two triangles are the same is whether one triangle can be repositioned on the other through any combination of slides, flips, or turns.

Through their experimentation, students should become aware of the *triangle inequality,* which states that the sum of the lengths of any two sides of a triangle must be greater than the length of the third side. If a group is not finding an impossible triangle, invent one—such as 3, 5, and 14—and give it to the group as a challenge.

During this time, students should be recording their measurements so they can share results later with the class. If a group is having trouble recording information, direct them back to your example or have them *briefly* observe another group that seems to be well-organized. Encourage students to make sketches of their triangles (with side lengths labeled) to help them look for interesting patterns.

Summarize

When students have done some exploration and addressed the questions about triangles, the whole-class discussion should clarify the principles that were revealed and give students a chance to share their insights.

Have groups make conjectures about what lengths will and will not make a triangle. Here are some conjectures students have made:

- Daniella said that two short sides added together have to be more than the longest side.

- Paul said that if the two short sides are less than the long side, they fall on top of each other.

- Yvonne said the two short sides cannot add up to the same as the long side or they won't stick up and leave any space inside.

Ask students to hypothesize about how the class's responses are alike and how they are different.

> Can we come up with a summary statement that would help someone who is not here today know how to judge whether three lengths will make a triangle without actually building the triangle?

As students add to the discussion, write the current summary statement on the board, and revise it as other students suggest improvements. Ask questions to stretch the students' thinking until you have a rule that clearly distinguishes lengths that will work from those that won't. One good way to push their thinking in a situation like this is to make up examples to test.

Students should leave Problem 2.1 with the ability to respond to the two questions posed in the problem. Answers should be more than just a yes or no; continue to pose questions that ask them to explain why certain lengths work and others do not.

When you feel students are ready to move on, look together at Problem 2.1 Follow-Up. These three questions focus on interesting characteristics of the triangles students have built. You might have the class look at the class data to find all of the triangles that are equilateral or isosceles or right, as these triangles are commonly used in designs and buildings. Then ask for examples of triangles that look very strange to the students. Their examples will probably be scalene triangles, in which none of the sides or angles are equal.

For question 3, you can have each group build one of their triangles to demonstrate symmetry. Discuss both line and turn symmetry for each of their examples. An equilateral triangle has three lines of symmetry, one from each vertex to the midpoint of the opposite side. An isosceles triangle has only one line of symmetry, from the vertex between the two equal sides to the center of the opposite side. An equilateral triangle also has turn symmetries of 120°, 180°, and 360°. Scalene triangles have only the trivial turn of 360° as a symmetry. When talking about turn symmetries, students might phrase their observations in other terms, such as, "You can turn the triangle one third of the way around and it will look the same."

As groups share information about their most interesting or unusual triangle, listen for misconceptions *and* for evidence of understanding. Do not press them for descriptions of angles (acute, obtuse, right) or for fancy side-length vocabulary (scalene, isosceles, equilateral).

2.2 • Building Quadrilaterals

In this problem, students use polystrips to build quadrilaterals. They discover a property similar to the triangle inequality: the sum of the lengths of the three shortest sides of a quadrilateral must be greater than the length of the longest side. They also discover that four side lengths do not determine a unique or stable shape.

Launch

This problem is similar to Problem 2.1, except that students will be building quadrilaterals instead of triangles.

> In the last problem, we looked at triangles and asked what the conditions were for any three lengths to make a triangle. We also asked whether three lengths that will make a triangle always make a *unique* triangle. In this problem, we will ask the same things about quadrilaterals. But, of course, it will take four lengths to try to build a quadrilateral.

Explain that groups will choose sets of four numbers to serve as the side lengths for the trials in their experiment. They will need to record their data—the lengths for any set they try and the results from that trial—in a chart. That way, they can quickly reconstruct examples to support what their group finds. They can use their recording scheme from the triangle problem as a model.

Explore

As you observe groups working, be sure students are using good recording strategies. If a group is not making much progress on the question of constructing more than one quadrilateral with a given set of four lengths, share something such as the following as a challenge.

> In another class, a group said they thought you could make more than one quadrilateral with the lengths 6, 8, 10, and 12. They said, "We put the 10 between the 6 and the 8, and the quadrilateral is different from the one we get when we put the 10 between the 8 and the 12." (*Demonstrate this with Polystrips.*) What do you think about this group's idea?

Summarize

In the class summary, key in on the two questions. Have the groups report their findings and build examples to support their conclusions. You want them to leave the experience not only able to explain what happened, but able to design a set of lengths that will provide evidence to support their findings.

For the question of uniqueness, a summary of strategies for finding different quadrilaterals from a given set of side lengths should arise from the discussion. Two powerful strategies, which focus on different aspects of what determines a quadrilateral, are these:

- Put the set of lengths together in different orders. (This technique highlights the role of *side lengths* in determining a shape.)

- Build a quadrilateral from Polystrips and then alter its angles by "squishing" the quadrilateral, which gives an infinite set of different shapes. (This technique highlights the role of *angles* in determining a shape.)

Discuss the questions in Problem 2.2 Follow-Up as a part of the summary.

As part of their homework, ask students to create quadrilaterals for the Launch for Problem 2.3. Give each student a sheet of isometric dot paper. Ask them to use a straightedge to draw two quadrilaterals—each about half a page—and carefully cut out the figures. They can color their quadrilaterals so they can be seen from a distance.

2.3 • Building Parallelograms

Many students come to grade 6 with misconceptions about shapes. Perhaps most confused is their understanding of what the various names for quadrilaterals mean. Most students have heard of and used the words *rectangle* and *square* but are unclear of the mathematical properties involved in those classifications. This problem deals with rectangles as a subset of parallelograms.

Launch

> ### For the Teacher: Defining Trapezoid
>
> Some of your students may know the word *trapezoid* for a quadrilateral with one set of parallel sides. The funny thing about this term is that mathematics texts do not agree on its definition. Some books do not allow parallelograms to be a special class of trapezoids (those with two pairs of parallel sides), but insist that one pair of sides must not be parallel. Other books use the inclusive classification, meaning that *trapezoid* is a large class that includes parallelograms, which includes rectangles, which includes squares. In this curriculum, an overemphasis on classification is not desirable, but if the interest arises from your students, you might want to discuss the issue of this definition.

Take time to see that your students gain more clarity about what it entails to be a quadrilateral, a parallelogram, a rectangle, and a square. One of the most effective ways for them to understand a concept is to see many examples that fit the concept and many that do not, which makes them think deeply about what the concept implies. The following activity is designed to help students sort out the meaning of *parallelogram*.

> We have been experimenting with Polystrips to discover important properties of triangles and quadrilaterals. In this problem, we will look at a special quadrilateral called a *parallelogram*. The basic question is, What makes a parallelogram a parallelogram?

> Some of you may know some things about parallelograms already. Jot those down on a piece of paper, and add to or revise your thinking as you go through the problem.

> Let's begin by organizing some data that will help us start to make sense of what a parallelogram is.

On the board, create a table with two columns, one labeled Parallelogram and the other labeled Not a Parallelogram.

We will be using the quadrilaterals you created last night and some that I have made as our data. I am going to call on you to tape your figure in the correct column. If you have a problem placing your figure, the rest of the class and I will help so that all of the data is placed correctly. Do I have a volunteer to get us started?

Be sure figures are placed correctly. When a few figures are on the board, stop and remind the class what they should be thinking about.

We now have some examples of parallelograms and nonparallelograms on the board. You should be writing down what you think makes a parallelogram. For each nonparallelogram, think about why it is not a parallelogram. Revise your description of a parallelogram to include any new ideas you get from additional figures that we place.

You will need to have a few parallelograms, rectangles, and squares to add to the data if none come from the students. You want the issue of whether a figure might have more than one name to come out of this launch. As interesting quadrilaterals are placed on the board, ask questions about other names they might have.

(Hold up a square.) Where do you think this should be placed on our data chart?

Let students voice their ideas. Place the figure in the Parallelogram column.

This is where the square goes. Does your preliminary definition of a parallelogram work for a square? Does a square have the characteristics you have said are necessary?

Does a square have some more things going for it that other parallelograms do not necessarily have? Is this a problem?

What are all the names you know for this figure?

You want students to begin to see that parallelograms are like many things in the world: they share certain characteristics with one another, but are not all exactly alike. People, for example, have special characteristics—old, young, red hair, brown eyes, long hair, six fingers—but are all *people*. You are not after a specific definition of parallelogram; you just want the issues to be raised and each student to have some conjectures written down in preparation for Problem 2.3. When you feel students have reached this point, review the problem with them, and turn them loose to explore the questions.

Explore

Have students work together in groups of two or three. Give students time to read Problem 2.3 and to use Polystrips to explore the relationships between rectangles and parallelograms. Check for understanding as you observe what various groups are doing. Ask questions that encourage students to better articulate what characteristics a parallelogram must have.

Summarize

In the class summary, let students share their thinking. Work toward agreement on a list of characteristics that students will include in their journals.

Ask about the special parallelograms. Polystrips are a wonderful tool to show in a dynamic way that if the opposite side lengths are the same, no matter how we change the angles, we still have a parallelogram. This helps students to see the square as just one "setting" of the size of the angles for a quadrilateral with all sides the same length.

There are many possible correct observations that students can make here, including these:

- Parallelograms have four sides and four angles

- Parallelograms have opposite sides that are parallel.

- Parallelograms have opposite angles that are equal.

- Parallelograms have opposite sides that are equal.

Additional Answers

Answers to Problem 2.2 Follow-Up

1. Students will probably identify rectangles and squares as common quadrilaterals. For these two figures, side lengths and angles are important: all angles must be 90° and, for a square, all sides must be equal. Take every opportunity to expand the students' thinking. For example, something as simple as making a square from Polystrips and rotating it until a vertex is at the top will lead to interesting discussion: the students see a diamond, and many will conclude that the figure is no longer a square. Students build inappropriate concepts about geometric figures because we seldom present figures in anything other than a standard position.

2. Students will probably focus on examples with little, if any, regularity. The sides may all be different lengths. One side may be very long relative to the others, producing a long, skinny figure.

3. Students are likely to suggest rectangles and squares; some may suggest isosceles trapezoids. These figures all have line symmetry. The square has four lines of symmetry—two joining the midpoints of opposite sides and two joining opposite corners—over which the figure can be flipped. The rectangle has only two lines of symmetry—those connecting the midpoints of the opposite sides. The isosceles trapezoid has only one line of symmetry—the line joining the midpoints of the two parallel sides. Every figure has the trivial 360° turn symmetry. However, some figures have more interesting turn symmetries. For example, a square also has 90°, 180°, 270°, and 360° turn symmetry, and a rectangle has 180° and 360° turn symmetry.

INVESTIGATION 3

Polygons and Angles

The shape of a polygon is determined as much by the measures of its angles as by the lengths of its sides. In this investigation, students develop an understanding of and skill in angle measurement.

Problem 3.1, Follow the Dancing Bee, suggests that it is common to think about angles in at least three different ways: as turns or rotations, as wedges or angular regions, and as the union of two rays with a common endpoint. We do not formally define *angle*. This informality allows us to address some important aspects of angles such as directed angles of more than 180°.

In Problem 3.2, Estimating Angle Measures, and Problem 3.3, Developing More Angle Benchmarks, students use bench-marks—starting with 90°—to estimate angle measures and to sketch angles. In Problem 3.4, Playing Four in a Row, students are introduced to another way to locate points in a plane by playing a tic-tac-toe game on a circular grid.

Problem 3.5, Using an Angle Ruler, introduces students to the angle ruler. Problem 3.6, Analyzing Measuring Errors, uses the example of Amelia Earhart's historic crash to demonstrate that imprecise angle measurements may have disastrous consequences.

Mathematical and Problem-Solving Goals

- **To develop an understanding of what an angle is and to find examples of angles in the real world**

- **To understand that the measure of an angle is the size of the opening or turn between its sides**

- **To learn that a full turn is divided into 360°, that a half turn measures 180°, and that a quarter turn measures 90°**

- **To estimate angle measures and to sketch angles using benchmarks**

- **To find precise angle measures using an angle ruler**

- **To use angles and angle measures in real-life applications**

Materials		
Problem	For students	For the teacher
All	Calculators	Transparencies 3.1 to 3.6 (optional)
3.2		Polystrips and brass fasteners (optional)
3.3	ShapesSet (1 per group)	
3.4	Labsheet 3.4 (1 each per student)	
3.5	Labsheet 3.5 (1 each per student), ShapesSet, angle rulers (1 per student)	Transparency of Labsheet 3.5
3.6	Labsheet 3.6 (1 each per student), angle rulers	

Follow the Dancing Bee

Launch

- Discuss the three ways to think about angles: as turns, as wedges, and as sides with a common vertex.

- Have students search the room for examples of turns, wedges, and sides.

Explore

- Encourage students to find more examples of turns, wedges, and sides as they work on the homework and throughout the unit.

- Designate a location for students to display the examples they find. (*optional*)

Summarize

- Over the next several days, as you work on other problems, take time to talk about the examples students find.

Assignment Choices

Unassigned choices from earlier problems

Polygons and Angles

If you experiment with making polygons, you will quickly see that there is more to a shape than the lengths of its sides. For example, with ten line segments of equal length, you can build a regular decagon or a five-point star. How are these two polygons different? *It's all in the angles!*

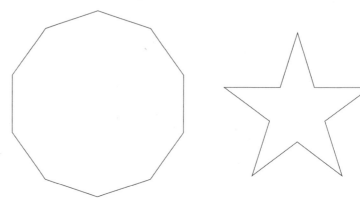

To describe polygons accurately, you must measure the **angles** formed where the sides of the polygon meet.

3.1 Follow the Dancing Bee

The workers in a honeybee hive fly great distances to find flowers with the nectar they need to make honey. When a bee finds a good patch of flowers, she returns to the hive and communicates the location of the flowers to the other bees. Scientific observation has shown that honeybees have an amazing method for giving directions from the hive to the flowers: they perform a lively dance!

During the direction dance, a honeybee moves in a combination of squiggly lines and half circles.

The squiggly lines in the dance indicate the direction of the flowers. If the flowers are in the direction of the sun, the bee dances in a line that is straight up and down.

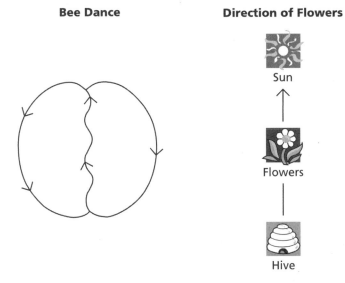

Bee Dance   **Direction of Flowers**

If the flowers are not in the direction of the sun, the bee dances in a tilted line. The angle of the tilt is the same as the angle formed by the sun, the hive, and the flowers.

Bee Dance   **Direction of Flowers**

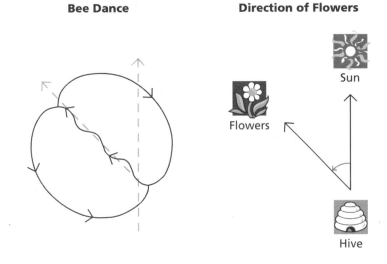

The bee dance illustrates one way that you can think about an angle—as a *turn*. When the honeybee dances along a tilted line, she is telling the other bees how far to *turn* from the sun to find the flowers.

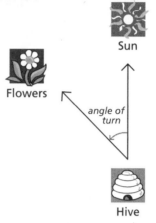

You can also think about an angle as a *wedge*, like a piece of pizza. Finally, you can think about an angle as *two sides* that meet at a point, like branches on a tree.

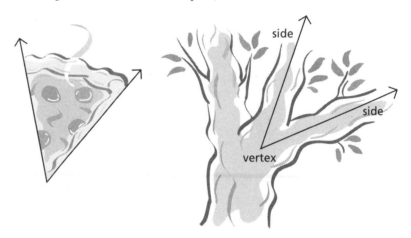

The point where the two sides touch is called the **vertex** of the angle. In the angle formed by the flowers, the hive, and the sun, the beehive is located at the vertex. The imaginary lines from the hive to the sun and from the hive to the flowers form the sides of the angle.

Estimating Angle Measures

Problem 3.1

Look around your school, your home, and the other buildings and landscapes you see around you to find examples of angles. Find at least one example of each type of angle described.

A. An angle that occurs as the result of a *turning motion*, such as the opening of a door

B. An angle that occurs as a *wedge*, such as a piece of pizza

C. An angle that occurs as *two sides* with a *common vertex*, such as the branches on a tree

Explain where you found each angle, and make a sketch of the figure in which each angle appears. Be ready to share your findings with the class.

■ **Problem 3.1 Follow-Up**

Determine whether each angle you found is a **right angle**—with sides that meet to form a square corner—or whether it is bigger or smaller than a right angle.

(3.2) **Estimating Angle Measures**

There are several ways to describe the size of an angle. The most common way is the **degree.** An angle of 1 degree (also written 1°) is a very small turn, or a very narrow wedge.

1°

The size of a degree was chosen so that a right angle has a measure of 90°. Here is a 90° angle. Imagine 90 copies of the 1° angle fitting into this angle.

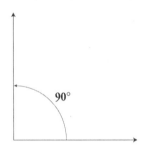

90°

Launch

■ Review the concept of a right angle.

■ Introduce the system of using degree measurements to identify angles.

Explore

■ Have students work in groups to sketch angles with measures that are close to the degree measures given.

■ As you circulate, check the reasonableness of their drawings.

Summarize

■ Check students' work, or have them check their own work against a transparency of the answers.

■ Discuss why 90° might have been chosen as the measure of a right angle. (*optional*)

■ Talk about the idea that the turn between two rays—not the length of the rays—determines the angle measure.

Answers to Problem 3.1

A. Possible answers: a car or bike changing direction; members of a marching band making turns; swinging of a baseball bat or golf club

B. Possible answers: pizza or pie sections; light from a flashlight; the tip of a pencil; my nose (with the tip as the vertex)

C. Possible answers: the edges of a floor, ceiling, or window; the hands of a clock; the blades of an open pair of scissors; two fingers spread apart

Answers to Problem 3.1 Follow-Up

Answers will vary.

Assignment Choices

ACE questions 13–18, 27–29, and unassigned choices from earlier problems

Here is an angle formed by one half the turn of a right angle. It measures 45°.

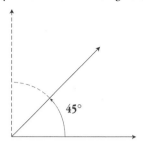

45°

It is often useful to *estimate* the measures of angles and to sketch angles when a measurement is given.

Problem 3.2

Sketch and find the degree measures of the angles made by these turns. For each sketch, include an arrow indicating the angle of turn.

A. One third of a right-angle turn   **B.** Two thirds of a right-angle turn

C. One quarter of a right-angle turn   **D.** One and one half right-angle turns

E. Two right-angle turns   **F.** Three right-angle turns

The angle below has a measure of about 120°. In G–L, make sketches of angles with *approximately* the given measure. For each sketch, include an arrow indicating the angle of turn.

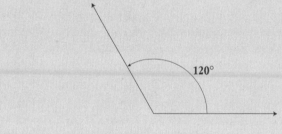

120°

G. 20°   **H.** 70°

I. 150°   **J.** 180°

K. 270°   **L.** 360°

Answers to Problem 3.2

See page 41j.

Answers to Problem 3.2 Follow-Up

The first angle is the largest, the second angle is the smallest, and the third angle is a right angle. Students' reasoning will vary.

Problem 3.2 Follow-Up

When you measure an angle, it is important to keep in mind what is being measured. For example, the sides of the 1° angle shown on page 25 are very long, but a 1° angle is a very small angle. The sides of angles are *rays*, lines that continue in one direction forever. For a given angle, you can draw the sides as long or as short as you wish. The size of an angle is *the amount of turn* from one side to another.

Which of the angles below is the largest? Which is the smallest? Which is a right angle? Explain your reasoning.

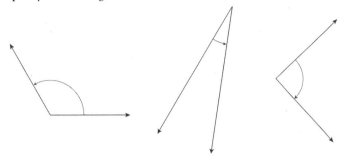

3.3 Developing More Angle Benchmarks

In Problem 3.2, you used a 90° angle as a *benchmark*, or reference, to help you sketch angles and estimate angle measures. The angles of some of the polygons in your Shapes Set can be other useful benchmarks.

Problem 3.3

Estimate and record the measure of each angle of shapes A, B, D, M, R, and V in your Shapes Set. Copy the shapes onto a sheet of paper, and label each angle with its measure.

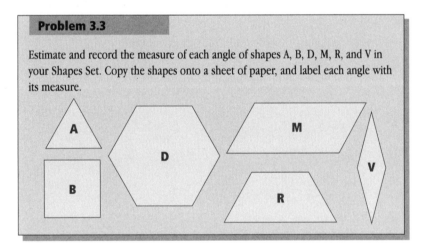

Answers to Problem 3.3

A (triangle): The measure of each angle is 60°.

B (square): The measure of each angle is 90°.

D (hexagon): The measure of each angle is 120°.

V (rhombus): The measure of each small angle is 30°. The measure of each large angle is 150°.

M (parallelogram): The measure of each small angle is 60°. The measure of each large angle is 120°.

R (trapezoid): The measure of each small angle is 60°. The measure of each large angle is 120°.

3.3

Developing More Angle Benchmarks

At a Glance

Grouping:
Small Groups

Launch

■ Ask questions about the angles in the shapes to start students thinking about comparing the angles to estimate their measures.

Explore

■ Have students work in groups to estimate the angles and record their measures.

■ As you circulate, look for interesting ways students are thinking about the problem.

Summarize

■ As a class, share strategies used for estimating angle measures.

■ Display the results for students to refer to throughout the unit. (*optional*)

Assignment Choices

ACE questions 19–26 (estimates only), and unassigned choices from earlier problems

■ Problem 3.3 Follow-Up

Use what you have learned about the measures of the angles in your Shapes Set to estimate the measures of the angles below.

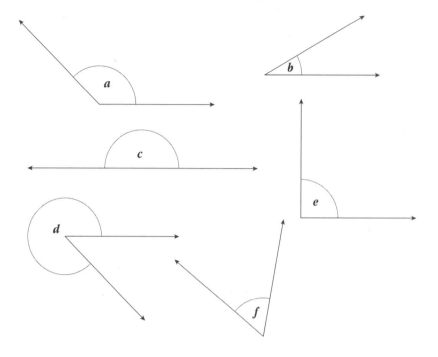

Answers to Problem 3.3 Follow-Up

Angle *a* = 135°; Angle *b* = 30°; Angle *c* = 180°; Angle *d* = 315°; Angle *e* = 90°; Angle *f* = 60°

3.4 Playing Four in a Row

You know how to locate points on a grid by using ordered pairs of coordinates. To locate a point, you can think of starting at (0, 0), moving over the number of units given by the first coordinate, and then moving up the number of units given by the second coordinate. On the grid at right, point A has coordinates (1, 4), point B has coordinates (3, 2), and point C has coordinates (5, 6).

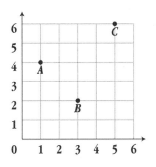

Mathematicians and scientists find it useful to locate points in other ways. One way to locate points is to use a circular grid. On this kind of grid, angle measures help describe the location of points.

Two examples of this kind of grid are shown below. They look very different from the grid shown above. The grid on the left has lines at 45° intervals. The grid on the right has lines at 30° intervals. The circles are numbered, moving out from the center at 0.

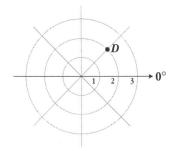 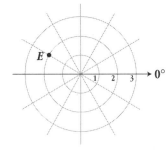

Points on these grids are described by giving a distance and an angle. For example, point D above has coordinates (2, 45°). To locate a point on one of these grids, start at the center of the grid and move over the number of units indicated by the first coordinate. Then, move along that circle the number of degrees given by the second coordinate. So to locate (2, 45°), move over to 2 on the 0° line and then move up to the 45° line. Can you find the coordinates of point E above?

In this problem, you will play a game called Four in a Row. The game can be played by two players or two teams.

At a Glance

Grouping: Pairs

Launch

- Review rectangular coordinates and ordered pairs.

- Introduce the idea of locating points on a circular grid.

- Have the whole class play a game of Four in a Row.

Explore

- Have students play Four in a Row and record any winning strategies they discover.

- As you circulate, check that students are using the grid correctly.

Summarize

- Discuss winning strategies students have found.

- Focus the discussion on what students have learned about angles.

Assignment Choices

ACE question 43 and unassigned choices from earlier problems

Have students play Four in a Row against someone at home, using strategies they learned in class.

Using an Angle Ruler

At a Glance

Grouping: Individuals

Launch

- Introduce the use of the angle ruler, and, as a class, practice both methods of measuring with it.

- Discuss the idea that all measurements are approximations.

Explore

- Circulate as students measure the angles in the shapes and compare their measurements to their earlier estimates.

- Have students show line symmetries with dotted lines. (*optional*)

Summarize

- Discuss the differences between estimates and measurements and the symmetries in the shapes.

- Talk about how the angles in these shapes relate to their ability to tile a plane.

Assignment Choices

ACE questions 1–4, 5–12, 30–35, 38–42, and unassigned choices from earlier problems

---

Four in a Row Rules

Four in a Row is played on a circular grid. Players take turns saying the coordinates of a point aloud and then marking the point on the grid. One player uses X's, and the other uses O's. Marks can be placed only on points on the grid where circles and sides meet. The winner is the first player to get four in a row along a line or around a circle. While one player takes a turn, the other player should listen carefully. A player must give correct coordinates before he or she can mark a point on the grid.

> #### Problem 3.4
>
> Play Four in a Row several times. Play games with both the 30° grid and the 45° grid on Labsheet 3.4. Write down any winning strategies you discover.

Problem 3.4 Follow-Up

Work with your partner to make up new rules for playing the game or to create a different board on which to play the game.

3.5 Using an Angle Ruler

In many situations in which distance and angles are measured, estimates are good enough. But sometimes it is important to measure very precisely. If you were navigating an ocean liner, an airplane, or a rocket, you would not want to just estimate the angles needed to plot your course.

There are several tools that help with angle measurement. One of the easiest to use is the *angle ruler*. An angle ruler has two arms, like the sides of an angle. The arms are joined by a rivet that allows them to swing apart to form angles of various sizes. The rivet is at the center of a circular ruler whose edge is marked with numbers from 0° to 360°.

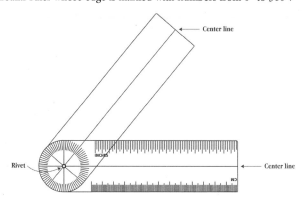

Answer to Problem 3.4 Follow-Up

Variations might include playing for only three in a row; allowing three or four marks in a spiral pattern to be a winning combination; adding another circle to the grid; and excluding the origin as a possible move. Students could also allow a player to capture a point marked by another player by naming the point with a different pair of coordinates. Each point can be named an infinite number of ways if negative coordinates or coordinates greater than 360° are allowed.

To measure an angle with an angle ruler, place the rivet over the vertex of the angle and set the center line of the arm passing through 0° on one side of the angle. Then swing the other arm around until its center line lies on the second side of the angle. The center line on the second arm will pass over a mark on the circular ruler, telling you the degree measure of the angle.

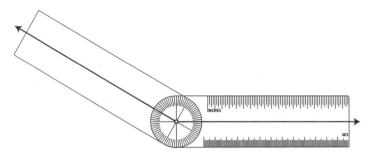

When you are measuring an angle on a wedge of some thickness, such as a block, you can place the object between the two arms of the angle ruler and read off the size of the angle, as shown here.

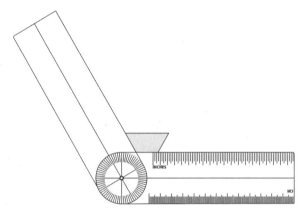

3.6

Analyzing Measuring Errors

At a Glance

Grouping:
Small Groups

Launch

- As a class, measure angles with measures that are not multiples of 5°.

- Have students discuss what might account for the differences in their results.

- Tell the story of Amelia Earhart's historic crash.

Explore

- Circulate as groups discuss the problem, make their measurements, and work on the follow-up.

- Have students display their data on the board or make a transparency of their solution. (optional)

Summarize

- Discuss groups' findings for the Earhart problem.

- As a class, analyze the measurements found for the six angles in the follow-up.

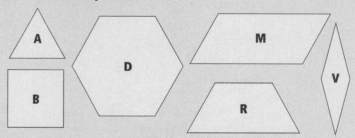
■ **Problem 3.5 Follow-Up**

In each shape you measured, what kinds of symmetry do you find?

3.6 Analyzing Measuring Errors

In 1937, the famous aviator Amelia Earhart tried to become the first woman to fly around the world. She began her journey on June 1, when she took off from Miami, Florida. She reached Lae, New Guinea, and then headed east toward Howland Island in the Pacific Ocean. She never arrived at Howland Island.

Assignment Choices

Unassigned choices from earlier problems

Assessment

It is appropriate to use Check-Up 1 after this problem.

Answers to Problem 3.5

See page 41j.

Answers to Problem 3.5 Follow-Up

Observations will vary greatly depending on the depth of understanding the students have for symmetry. They may observe that all shapes except the parallelogram have line symmetry and that all shapes except the trapezoid have turn symmetry. Symmetry has not been developed much in the unit, so you will need to decide how much time to invest here. (We return to symmetry in the *Ruins of Montarek* unit on spatial visualization.)

In 1992, 55 years later, investigators found evidence that Earhart had crashed on the desert island of Nikumaroro, far off her intended course. Her navigator had apparently made errors in plotting the course. When flying long distances, even small errors can lead a flight far astray.

Did you know?

Amelia Earhart's tragic flight was not her first attempt to circle the globe. On March 17, 1937, she took off from Oakland, California, heading west around the world. Three days later, upon takeoff from Hawaii, her plane made a sharp, uncontrollable turn on the runway causing the landing gear to collapse and damaging the underside of her plane.

Every time we use a measurement tool, there is some error. No instrument gives absolutely precise measurements. Why is this?

The map on the following page shows Lae, New Guinea, Howland Island, and Nikumaroro Island. You can use the map and an angle ruler, to measure the angles involved in Earhart's flight.

Problem 3.6

How many degrees off course was Earhart's crash site from her intended destination?

Problem 3.6 Follow-Up

1. Use your angle ruler to measure the six angles in Problem 3.3 Follow-Up on page 28. (You have already estimated the angle measurements.)

2. Look at your measures and your estimates from Problem 3.3 Follow-Up. If there are differences, explain why.

Answer to Problem 3.6

On the map, the crash site is about 8° from Howland Island.

Answers to Problem 3.6 Follow-Up

1. Angle a = 135°; Angle b = 30°; Angle c = 180°; Angle d = 315°; Angle e = 90°; Angle f = 60°

2. Answers will vary.

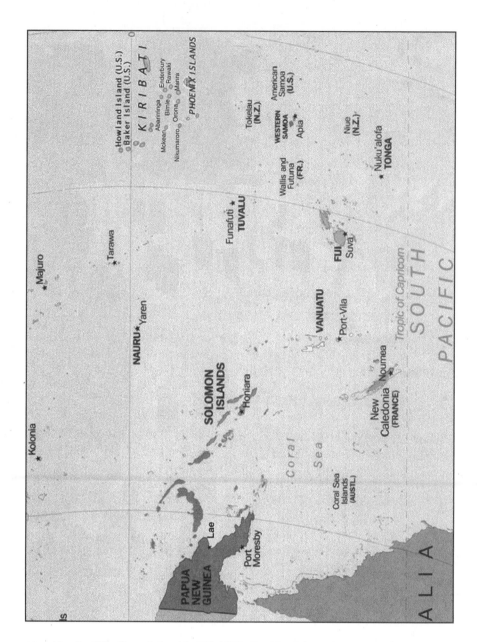

Adapted from Small Blue Planet. © Copyright 1993–1995 by Now What? Software, San Francisco. This map was created from original maps made by the Central Intelligence Agency and the Defense Mapping Agency.

Applications • Connections • Extensions

As you work on these ACE questions, use your calculator whenever you need it.

Applications

In 1–4, estimate the measures of the angles of the following bee dances. Then check your estimates by using an angle ruler.

1.

2.

3.

4.

In 5–12, draw angles with the given measures.

5. 45°   **6.** 70°   **7.** 110°   **8.** 170°

9. 200°   **10.** 270°   **11.** 20°   **12.** 180°

Investigation 3: Polygons and Angles **35**

11.

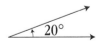

12.

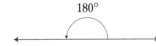
180°

Answers

Applications

1. approximately 30°
2. approximately 45°
3. approximately 90°
4. approximately 133°
5.

6.

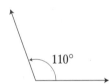

7.

8.

170°

9.

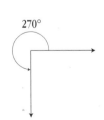
200°

10.

270°

11. See left.
12. See left.

Investigation 3 **35**

13. 90°
14. 180°
15. 270°
16. 45°
17. 30°
18. 360°
19. g
20. d
21. b
22. h
23. c
24. a
25. f
26. e

In 13–18, give the degree measures of each turn.

13. One right-angle turn
14. Two right-angle turns
15. Three right-angle turns
16. One half of a right-angle turn
17. One third of a right-angle turn
18. Four right-angle turns

In 19–26, *without* using an angle ruler, determine the letter of the angle below with a measure closest to the measure given. Check your answers with an angle ruler.

19. 30°   **20.** 60°   **21.** 90°   **22.** 120°
23. 150°   **24.** 180°   **25.** 270°   **26.** 350°

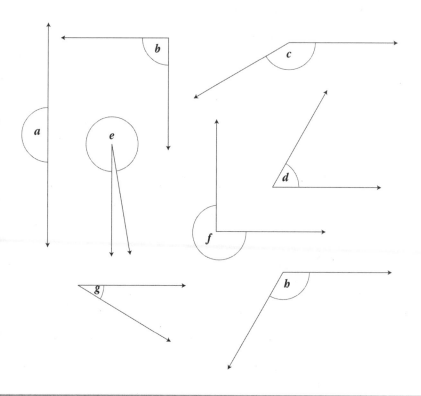

In 27–29, determine whether the angles are the same size. If they are not, tell which angle is larger.

27.

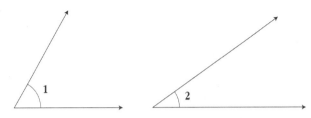

28.

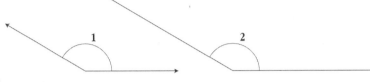

29.

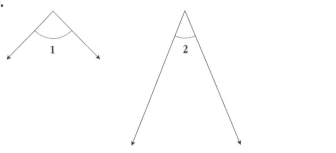

At the start of each hour, the minute hand of a clock points straight up, at the 12. In 30–35, determine the angle through which the minute hand passes as the given amount of time passes. Make a sketch to illustrate each situation.

30. 15 minutes   **31.** 30 minutes   **32.** 20 minutes

33. 1 hour   **34.** 5 minutes   **35.** $1\frac{1}{2}$ hours

Investigation 3: Polygons and Angles   **37**

27. Angle 1 is larger.

28. The two angles are nearly identical.

29. Angle 1 is larger.

30. 90°

31. 180°

32. 120°

33. 360°

34. 30°

35. 540°

Connections

36. Answers will vary.

37. Answers will vary.

38a. Possible answer: Average the measures and then make small adjustments because you want the angles to add to 180°.

38b. Students may choose to compute means, medians, or modes for the measures given. Computing the means gives measures of 52°, 36.7°, and 89.7°. Finding the modes gives measures of 50°, 35°, and 90°. Finding the medians gives measures of 52°, 36°, and 90°.

38c. See page 41k.

Connections

36. Describe two situations in which angle measurements are used. Find one situation where very precise measurement is important and another situation where an estimate will be good enough.

37. Describe two situations in which length measurements are used. Find one situation where very precise measurement is important and another situation where an estimate will be good enough.

38. Here are the results ten students got when they measured the angles of the triangle below:

Angle *A*: 52°, 53°, 55°, 50°, 52°, 50°, 55°, 50°, 53°, 50°

Angle *B*: 37°, 35°, 35°, 35°, 40°, 40°, 37°, 35°, 35°, 38°

Angle *C*: 90°, 90°, 89°, 90°, 88°, 92°, 86°, 91°, 91°, 90°

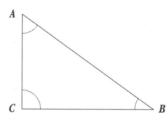

a. What method would you use to decide on the best measurement for each angle?

b. What degree measure will your method give for each angle?

c. Make line plots of the data for each angle, and explain how your choices of best measurements relate to the patterns in those plots.

39. This circle is divided into wedges formed by angles with vertices at the center of the circle. Such angles are called **central angles** of the circle. The central angles shown here each measure 90°.

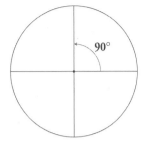

In a–c, sketch a circle divided into the given number of equal wedges, and find the measure of the central angles.

a. 8 equal pieces   **b.** 6 equal pieces   **c.** 3 equal pieces

d. What other ways could you cut a circle into equal wedges to give central angles with whole-number degree measurements? List the number of pieces and the measure of each central angle.

40. Measure each interior angle in the decagon and the star below. Look for patterns relating the angle measures in the two figures. Compare the lengths of the sides. What do you notice?

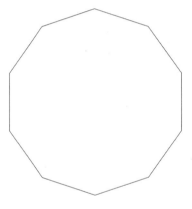

41. How do the perimeters (distance around) of the two figures in question 40 relate to each other?

39a. 45°

39b. 60°

39c. 120°

39d. The circle can be divided into 1 wedge of 360°, 2 wedges of 180°, 3 wedges of 120°, 4 wedges of 90°, 5 wedges of 72°, 6 wedges of 60°, 8 wedges of 45°, 9 wedges of 40°, 10 wedges of 36°, 12 wedges of 30°, 15 wedges of 24°, 18 wedges of 20°, 20 wedges of 18°, 24 wedges of 15°, 30 wedges of 12°, 36 wedges of 10°, 40 wedges of 9°, 45 wedges of 8°, 60 wedges of 6°, 72 wedges of 5°, 90 wedges of 4°, 120 wedges of 3°, 180 wedges of 2°, 360 wedges of 1°.

40. In the decagon, each interior angle is very close to 144°. In the star, the interior angles alternate between 36° and 252°. In both figures, the angle sum is 1440°. All the sides in both figures have the same length.

41. The perimeters of the two figures are equal.

Extensions

42. This exercise illustrates the general property that if a family of parallel lines is cut by a transversal, corresponding angles are the same size.

42a. On the left, all lines are perpendicular to the transversal, so all angles are 90°. On the right, the acute angles are 45° and the obtuse angles are their supplements, or 135°.

42b. The angles are either the same or their measures add to 180°.

42c. Possible answers: The left pattern occurs in Venetian blinds, siding on a house, and notebook paper. The right pattern occurs where railroad tracks cross streets at an angle.

43. Answers will vary. Student grids may have small angles and have many possible points to capture or on large angles that have fewer points to capture.

44. Looking at polygons highlights what an interesting object a circle is. A circle has no sides or angles, yet it is marvelously symmetric. Any turn around the center is a symmetry. This makes a circle roll smoothly, rather than with the strange bumpy motion a polygon would have. This also makes the circle a universal cap or lid for containers, as it will fit a container in any turn position. Spherical balls have no protrusions to cause funny bounces.

Extensions

42. Below are two sets of parallel lines cut by another line.

   a. In each drawing, measure the angles formed where the single line cuts across each of the parallel lines.

   b. Describe any patterns you notice in the angle measurements.

   c. Look around your school and your home to find places where similar patterns are formed. Sketch and describe some of the patterns you discover.

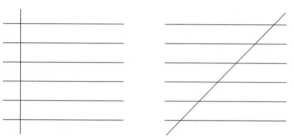

43. Design a new circular grid for playing Four in a Row. Play your game with a friend or a member of your family. Explain the ideas that led to your new design, and compare playing the game on the new grid to playing it on the grids you used in Problem 3.4.

44. Why are the wheels of bicycles, cars, and trains; the plates and glasses that we eat and drink from; the lids on bottles, jars, and cans; and the balls in many games we play round (not square or other polygon shapes)?

Mathematical Reflections

In this investigation, you thought about angles in several ways. You have become skilled at estimating measures of angles and using tools to make more precise measurements. These questions will help you summarize what you have learned:

1 Give examples of where angles occur as

    a. turns   **b.** wedges   **c.** sides with a common vertex

2 Explain what a *degree* is and how it is used to describe the size of an angle.

3 What is the importance of benchmark angles? How can they be used to make accurate estimates of angle measures?

4 Explain what an angle ruler is and how it can be used to measure the size of angles.

5 Name some situations in which angle measures must be precise. Name some other situations in which an estimate is all that is necessary.

Think about your answers to these questions, discuss your ideas with other students and your teacher, and then write a summary of your findings in your journal.

Don't forget to write about your new insights into angles! Are you remembering to collect examples of how shapes are used all around you?

Tip for the Linguistically Diverse Classroom

Original Rebus The Original Rebus technique is described in detail in *Getting to Know Connected Mathematics*. Students make a copy of the text before it is discussed. During discussion, they generate their own rebuses for words they do not understand as the words are made comprehensible through pictures, objects, or demonstrations Example: Item 1—key words for which students may make rebuses are *turns, wedges,* and *sides.*

Possible Answers

1a. tires, gates, clocks

1b. pie slices, pizzas, picture frames

1c. street maps, lines in designs, baselines in games

2. A degree is $\frac{1}{90}$ of a square corner. The measurement system for angles is based on subdividing a square corner into 90 equal turns. The measure of each of these small turns is 1°. This is like 1 inch in measuring length. To measure an angle, we need to figure out how many 1° angles are needed to match the angle.

3. Benchmark angles give us a quick way to estimate measurements. Using 90° and factors of 90°— such as 45°, 30°, 15°, or even 10°—we can make good estimates of the measures of all sorts of angles. The fact that we can reason with shapes from the Shapes Set to assign degrees to all of their angles shows that using benchmarks can help us.

4. An angle ruler is a tool that allows us to measure angles. We can either place the rivet on the vertex of the angle and align the centerlines of the arms with the angle's rays, or we can align the angle's rays with the insides of the arms.

5. In navigation and carpentry, we need precise measurements of angles. For slicing a pie or buying part of a round of cheese, we need only an estimate.

TEACHING THE INVESTIGATION

3.1 • Follow the Dancing Bee

This problem introduces students to three ways of thinking about angles: as turns, wedges, and sides. Students are asked to look for examples of angles and try to categorize them as turns, wedges, or sides. This will be the first mention of right angles in the student edition, though it may already have been a topic of discussion in your classroom.

Launch

Read the introduction to the problem aloud, and discuss with your students the different kinds of angles that occur in the world. Have them examine the room to find examples of each kind of angle. For example, the wooden part of a door between the top and one of the vertical sides might be called a *wedge*. The swinging or opening of the door might be seen as a *turn* through an angle. When a student holds the door open to talk with a friend before class begins, the door and the wall could be considered *sides* of an angle.

Explore

You want to get students thinking about angles as turns, wedges, and sides and help them start looking for examples outside of the classroom. Launch this problem, and then assign it for homework. Encourage students to continue to look for interesting angles in the world while they study the rest of the unit. To maintain interest, you may wish to designate a place in the classroom where students can display examples of what they are discovering. Because the Explore phase takes place over several days, move on to the next problem. You do not need to summarize before moving on.

Summarize

Make time to talk about this problem over the next several days as students bring in examples.

3.2 • Estimating Angle Measures

In this problem, students examine an angle with a measure of 1° and are introduced to the measurement of angles. This is the first time they are asked to use degree measures to identify angles; previously, they have only compared angles to a right angle, which was defined as a square corner. They now learn that a right angle has a measure of 90°, and they estimate from this benchmark to sketch other angles.

Launch

To begin, focus their attention on right angles.

> We all know what a square corner is. We also know that another name for a square corner is a *right angle*.

> Who can find a right angle in this room? Who can find an angle smaller than a right angle in this room? Who can find an angle greater than a right angle in this room?

Guide students to the idea of making comparisons.

> How can we tell when an angle is less than a right angle?

Students may suggest, for example, that you can just compare the angle to the corner of a sheet of paper.

Read the introduction to the problem, and focus students on the illustrations. Talk about the angle of a complete turn, which you can demonstrate by using two Polystrips and a connector and turning one of the strips 360°. Explain that the standard system of measuring angles breaks the turn into 360 small turns, each of which is 1° of turn. This means that a right angle must be 90°.

In this problem, knowing that a square corner is 90° allows students to estimate the degree measure of any angle by comparing it to a right angle. You might draw an angle on the board and have the class talk about whether it is larger, smaller, or equal to a right angle. Then ask the class to estimate how many degrees they think are in the measure of the angle. When a reasonable answer has been agreed on, have students work in groups of 2 or 3 on Problem 3.2. Although students are working in groups, have each student make his or her own set of drawings.

Explore

If students are having trouble estimating their angles, you might suggest that they draw a dotted line for 90° as a reference point and then make their angle side a solid line (refer them to the example on page 26 of the student edition). As you circulate, check that the groups' answers are reasonable. A student who draws a 100° angle to represent 70° is not making a reasonable estimate. Students should be able to make fairly good sketches of 45°, 30°, and 15°, for example, by finding half of a right angle, a third of a right angle, and half of a third of a right angle.

Remind students to label the angles in their sketches with degree measures and arrows indicating the angle of turn.

Summarize

There are many ways to check the groups' sketches. One possibility is to display a transparency of the correct angles for students to compare to their sketches. Or, you may want to hand out a copy of Transparency 3.2B to each group. Students could check their work by placing the transparency over their angles. Make sure students understand that their sketches do not have to be a perfect match.

You might want to have a class discussion about why 90° was chosen as the measure of a right angle. Maybe the key number is really 360°, which has many factors and can be divided in many ways.

For the Teacher: Babylonians and Angles

The ancient Babylonians established a convention of measuring angles in degrees. They set the measure of an angle that goes all the way around a point to 360°. They may have chosen 360° because their number system was based on the number 60. They may have also considered the fact that 360 has many factors.

You can use Problem 3.2 Follow-Up as a part of the summary. Emphasize to students that when we measure an angle, we are measuring the opening or turn between the sides of the angle. The lengths of the two sides (*rays*) that form the angle do not affect the measure of the angle. For example, these are all 30° angles:

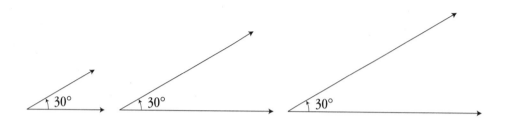

For the Teacher: Measuring Angles

The issue of the measure of an angle not being dependent on the lengths of its sides is an important one. Students often have a hard time remembering what is being measured when they measure an angle. In the upcoming problems, we confront this issue in a number of ways. In Problem 3.6, students will see that as they move further out along a ray, the distance to a corresponding point on the other ray does indeed increase. This problem gives you an opportunity to help students sort out what is being measured: the distance between points on opposite rays equidistant from the vertex increases, but the angle measure remains the same.

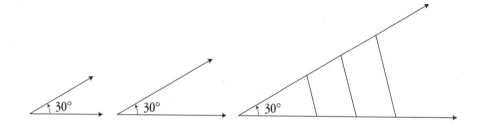

3.3 • Developing More Angle Benchmarks

This problem gives students practice in using angles they are familiar with (such as the right angle) to estimate the measures of other angles. The goals for this activity are to give students more practice with estimation and to increase their ability to reason with numbers and shapes.

Launch

In this activity, students use shapes A, B, D, M, R, and V, and combinations of these shapes, to find the measure of every angle in each shape.

Begin the activity by having students look through the indicated shapes as you ask some questions.

> Which angle on these six shapes is the smallest? Which angle is the largest?

> Can you find a 90° angle on one of these shapes? How do you know it is 90°?

> How does the largest angle of shape D compare to the right angle? Is it larger or smaller?

> What would be a reasonable estimate of the measure of the largest angle of shape D? How do you know this is reasonable?

When you are satisfied that students have some strategies to begin reasoning about the angles of the shapes, read or describe Problem 3.3.

Explore

Let students work in groups of two or three to estimate and to record their strategies for reasoning about the size of angles. Suggest that sketches may be used as part of the evidence to support their answers. As you work with the groups, look for interesting ways of reasoning that you want to be sure are shared in the summary.

Note: Students will actually measure these angles with angle rulers in Problem 3.5, so don't be too concerned with small inaccuracies; however, the inaccuracies should be minor considering the structure of the problem. Once students finish Problem 3.3, have them estimate the measures of the angles in the follow-up.

Summarize

Have students report their findings in a class discussion. Take time to explore all the strategies they used to arrive at their answers. You may want to display this benchmark information for students to refer to as they proceed through the unit. Here is one way a student worked with the square and the rhombus:

Roberto knew that the four angles of the square are each 90°. Using that benchmark, he placed the rhombus (shape V) on the square, aligning a vertex and side of one of the smaller rhombus angles with a vertex and side of the square. The angles did not match, but Roberto found that, by using two more rhombus shapes, three of the small angles together matched one angle of the square. He concluded that, since three of the rhombus angles were equal to 90°, a single angle measured 30°. He could now use the 30° angle to help him find the measures of other angles.

3.4 • Playing Four in a Row

In this problem, students play a tic-tac-toe game on a polar coordinate grid.

Launch

Briefly review rectangular coordinates and ordered pairs with your students. Refer them to the rectangular coordinate grid on page 29 of the student edition.

> In this problem, we are going to explore a different way of locating points.

Refer students to the two grids on page 29, or display Transparency 3.4. Point out that these grids have lines that form angles and circles. Have students look closely at the grid on the left.

> What are the measures of some of the angles in this grid? Look especially at angles with a vertex at the center of the grid.

Point out a 45° angle, a 90° angle, a 135° angle, and so on. Help students to see that the angles are all multiples of 45°.

> Using these grids, you describe a point by giving two numbers. The first number tells how far to move from the center of the grid. The second number tells the amount of turn measured in degrees. How would I find the point (3, 90°)?

Help students to see that to locate this point, you move out 3 units along the 0° line (x-axis) and then move through a turn of 90° along that circle. Playing the game as a class helps students learn how to locate other points on both grids and understand how the grids work. You can use one of the grids on Transparency 3.4.

> We are going to play a game of tic-tac-toe on this new grid. To win, you will need four marks in a row—although four in a row may mean around a circle or on a line. We will play the left half of the room against the right half. The left half of the room will be X's, and the right half will be O's. Can someone on the left side of the room give me the coordinates of a point on this grid?

When a student gives you a point, count out from the center for the first number, then measure the turn on the circle for the second number. Mark this with an X.

> Now I need someone on the right side of the room to give me the coordinates of a point.

Again, count out to the right from the center, then measure around the circle. Mark the intersection with an O. Continue until one team gets four in a row.

Explore

Hand out Labsheet 3.4, Four in a Row Game Boards. Have the students play the game in pairs or two against two. As you work with the groups, be sure they are using the grid appropriately. The game should increase students' estimation and reasoning skills with angles. Have them record any winning strategies they discover.

Summarize

Students can report on winning strategies they found or moves they hoped others would make to put them at an advantage. They should be able to discuss whether going first gives a noticeable advantage. Ask questions to focus the discussion on what they have learned about angles. Indicate a point on the grid.

> Tell me how to locate this point. What about this one?

You may want to create a different grid to use in the summary, such as one with rays at 15° intervals. Have students tell you how to find your way to points on that grid.

3.5 • Using an Angle Ruler

This problem introduces a measuring tool for angles that has a long history, especially in medicine, but little prior use in mathematics education. The angle ruler's formal name is *goniometer* (gō̄-nē-om´-i-ter), which means "angle measurer."

Launch

Instructions for using the angle ruler can be found on page 31 of the student edition. Use Labsheet 3.5, Angles and Polygons, to help explain how to use the angle ruler. Pass out a copy of the labsheet to each student, and display a transparency of the labsheet. Demonstrate how to measure one of the angles as students follow along at their desks. Have them measure two or three separate angles and a polygon with you and record the angle measures they read. Students will get slightly different measures, and this will allow you to talk about the fact that *all* measures are approximations. There is always some error in measurements we make, no matter how precise the tool we are using.

When you feel that students understand how to use the angle ruler by placing the vertex of the angle at the rivet, have them measure an angle they have already measured by aligning the angle's sides with the insides of the angle ruler's arms. Students should see that this method gives the same results except for errors of measurement.

For the Teacher: Using the Angle Ruler

This diagram illustrates why the gripping method gives the same results as placing the rivet over the vertex of the angle being measured. The overlap of the sides of the ruler form a rhombus as you separate them. In a rhombus, opposite angles are equal. This means that the rhombus angle at the rivet and the opposite angle are equal. The angle opposite the rivet in the rhombus is also equal to the angle between the sides since they are vertical angles (i.e. angles formed by two intersecting lines). So, when you place a shape between the arms of the ruler, the angle at the rivet has the same measure as the angle between the arms.

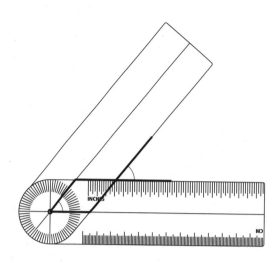

Explore

Have students work on Problem 3.5. Remind them to sketch each shape and to label its angles. When they have completed Problem 3.5, have them work on Problem 3.5 Follow-Up, which asks about the symmetries of the shapes. You may need to point out that symmetry is first presented on page 5. You may want to ask students to show line symmetries with dotted lines.

Summarize

Have students give the angle measure for each of the shapes. Discussing student responses to the questions in Problem 3.5 would be time well-spent.

Discuss Problem 3.5 Follow-Up. Students may have difficulty describing turn symmetries. This would be a good time to discuss turn symmetry by presenting some examples. You can demonstrate at the overhead projector using a copy of shape A cut from transparency film. Hold the triangle down by putting a pin through its center.

> If I put a pin in the equilateral triangle to hold the center in place, how can I turn the triangle so that it looks like its starting position?

Help the students to see that you can turn the triangle a third of a full turn, as shown below.

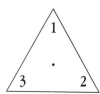
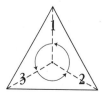
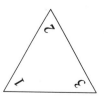

I can turn the triangle one third of a full turn, so that vertex 1 is at position 3, vertex 2 is at position 1, and vertex 3 is at position 2. The triangle looks like its starting position.

How can we tell what angle of turn this is?

Help students see that, since 360 ÷ 3 = 120, one third of a full 360° turn is 120°.

Can I turn the triangle some more to find another turn symmetry?

Help students to see that you can turn the triangle another third of a full turn. This is a 240° turn from its original position. You can also turn the triangle completely around, so vertex 1 is at the top. This is a 360° turn.

3.6 • Analyzing Measuring Errors

The big idea in this problem is knowing when precision in measurement is important. The Amelia Earhart story illustrates a situation in which a small measurement error made a life-and-death difference. What is deceptive about angles is that, while the degree measure of the angle does not change when we extend the rays that form the sides of the angle, the distance between the rays—measured from a point on one ray to the point the same distance from the vertex on the other ray—does increase (see the illustration on page 41c).

Launch

Up until now, students have used the angle ruler to measure angles that aligned with the ruler's 5° interval marks. In this problem, they need to measure between the 5° intervals.

Distribute Labsheet 3.6, Sheet of Angles. Have students measure the four angles and record the numbers of degrees they find. Then ask them to compare their results with a partner's results and to discuss what might account for differences they found. Students do not need to agree on the degree measurements, but their measurements should be close and their discussion should help one another understand the issues involved in making precise measurements. Guide the class in reaching this understanding.

How do you decide the number of degrees for angles between the 5° intervals on the ruler?

What things do you check to make sure you are making accurate measurements?

Be sure students notice the extra scale on the measuring circle of the angle ruler, which helps the user to measure with greater accuracy. For a quick check, display the angles with their measures, and ask whether students have any questions about any of the measures.

Use the text in the student edition or additional resources to tell the story of the Amelia Earhart crash. Focus students on the issues raised in the problem, and let them work in groups to explore the map and the questions.

Explore

While groups are measuring and discussing the problem and the follow-up questions, you may want to start collecting their answers on the board for discussion during the summary. As students check the accuracy of their own work, allow them to go to the board and revise their answers. (Having students initial their data as they place it on the board will avoid distracting discussions of the "they changed our data" sort.) Since it may take some time to summarize the follow-up, you may want groups to make transparencies of their solution or record them on large sheets of paper so they have something visual with which to "argue" their point.

Summarize

Have group representatives report on the findings of their group (if you have chosen to use transparencies or large sheets of paper, let them "show and tell").

Because it takes a long time to collect, organize, display, and interpret the data, some teachers handle Problem 3.6 Follow-Up in the following manner:

- The teacher makes six columns on the board with the headings Angle *a* through Angle *f*.
- Students list their measurements for angles *a* through *f* on the board.
- The teacher divides the class into six groups and assigns each group the task of organizing the data for one of the angles, displaying the organized data on a transparency, and finding the range and measures of center for their data set.
- Each group reports its findings to the class.

You might suggest that the groups make line plots of the data, such as the following:

```
                        X
                        X
                        X
                        X                   X
                        X                   X
                        X                   X
                        X    X              X
                        X    X              X
                   X    X    X              X
         X         X    X    X    X         X
         X    X    X    X    X    X    X    X
        ─────────────────────────────────────
        128  129  130  131  132  133  134  135
```

Each number represents an angle measure, and each X represents a student who found that measure. Students can find the mean of the data and the mode (the value that occurs most frequently). If students know how to find the median, they can find that as well. Students might also talk about the range of the data and the size of the possible error in the measurement. (Line plots and measures of center are discussed in the *Data About Us* unit.)

Additional Answers

Answers to Problem 3.2

A.
30°

B.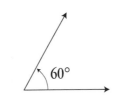
60°

C.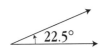
22.5°

D.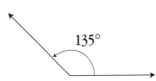
135°

E.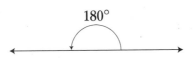
180°

F.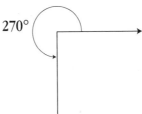
270°

G.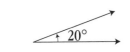
20°

H.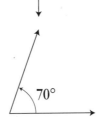
70°

I.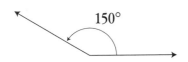
150°

J.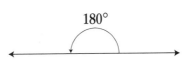
180°

K.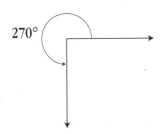
270°

L.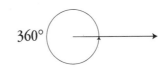
360°

Answers to Problem 3.5

A. Answers will vary, but students should realize that measurements made with an angle ruler are probably more accurate.

B. Since the hexagon, square, and triangle are regular, the measure of the angles within each is the same—120°, 90°, and 60° respectively. The measures of the two small angles of the trapezoid and parallelogram are each 60°. The two large angles of the trapezoid and parallelogram each measure 120°. Opposite angles of the rhombus measure 30° and 150°.

C. The hexagon, trapezoid, and parallelogram each have 120° angles. The triangle, trapezoid, and parallelogram each have 60° angles.

D. Students should recognize that there are 360° around each vertex point in a tiling, so each of these six shapes can be used to make a tiling. The students may see that some figures can be used together because their angle measures are the same or one measure is a factor of another, and the measures of the angles are factors of 360°.

ACE Answers

Connections

38c. Explanations of how the line plots relate to the student's choice of the best measurements will vary.

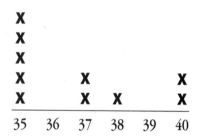

```
X
X
X        X   X        X
X        X   X        X
──────────────────────────
50   51  52  53  54   55
```

```
X
X
X
X        X            X
X        X   X        X
──────────────────────────
35   36  37  38  39   40
```

```
                     X
                     X
                     X   X
X            X   X   X   X   X
──────────────────────────────────
85   86  87  88  89  90  91  92
```

Polygon Properties and Tiling

The ideas in Investigation 4 are presented in a context about which students are already curious: the amazing patterns in the behavior of bees. The principle goal of the first investigation was to pose the problem of *which* shapes can be used to tile a surface. The principle goal of this investigation is to discover *why* these shapes can tile a surface, while others cannot.

Problem 4.1, Relating Sides to Angles, explores the relationships between the number of sides and the angle measures of regular polygons. In Problem 4.2, Measuring Irregular Polygons, students discover that the angle sum of any polygon can be predicted from the number of sides it has. In Problem 4.3, Back to the Bees!, students explore how the angle measures of a polygon determine whether it will tile a plane.

This investigation follows the work with angles so students can reason about whether there is an exact "fit" of polygons around a vertex point in a tiling. Students should see the connection between a full turn of 360° and the number of degrees in the sum of the angles around a vertex point. They will be able to find the number of degrees in the angles of regular polygons and to construct convincing arguments that the angles fit exactly around a vertex point. This work with tiling reinforces students' understanding of angles, their measures, and their importance in design.

Mathematical and Problem-Solving Goals

- **To use information about angles to test potential tiling patterns**

- **To understand why and to show how any triangle can be used to tile**

- **To understand why squares, rectangles, parallelograms, and other quadrilaterals of any shape can be used to tile**

- **To show how regular hexagons can be used to tile**

- **To understand that most other polygons do not tile**

- **To understand that circular shapes do not tile**

Materials		
Problem	**For students**	**For the teacher**
All	Calculators	Transparencies 4.1 to 4.3 (optional)
4.1	Angle rulers	
4.2	Labsheet 4.2 (optional), straightedges (rulers or strips of tagboard), scissors	
4.3	ShapeSet (1 per group)	ShapeSet for use on overhead projector (optional: copy the blackline masters onto transparency film)

Student Pages 42–50   **Teaching the Investigation 50a–50i**

Relating Sides to Angles

At a Glance

**Grouping:
Small Groups**

Launch

- Remind students of their earlier work with regular polygons.

- Help students to see that as the number of sides in a polygon increases, the size of the interior angles increases.

Explore

- Circulate as groups measure the polygons, organize their data, and look for patterns relating the number of sides to the measure of the interior angles and the angle sum.

Summarize

- As a class, refine data and make a chart of the class's findings.

- Encourage students to find patterns in the chart.

- Have students explore the relationship of side length to angle size.

Polygon Properties and Tiling

The shape of a polygon depends on the number of sides it has, the length of those sides, and the size of its angles. In order to see how sides and angles are related in polygons, you can gather some data from polygons, organize the data, and look for patterns. Patterns in the angle measures of regular polygons help to explain why hexagons show up in honeycombs.

4.1 Relating Sides to Angles

Below are six regular polygons that are already familiar to you. All of the sides in all of the polygons are the same length. The angles where the sides meet are clearly not the same in all the figures. What pattern do you see in the sizes of the interior angles as the number of sides increases?

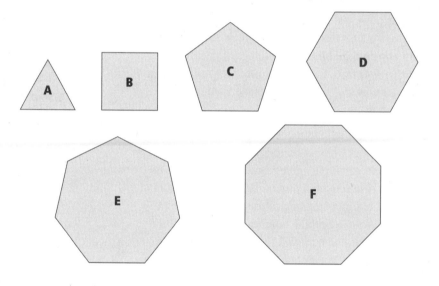

Assignment Choices

ACE question 1 and unassigned choices from earlier problems

In preparation for Problem 4.2, you could have students draw a variety of irregular triangles and quadrilaterals. They should be drawn with a straightedge and large enough to measure easily.

Answers to Problem 4.1

A.

Polygon	Number of sides	Interior angle	Angle sum
Triangle	3	60°	180°
Square	4	90°	360°
Pentagon	5	108°	540°
Hexagon	6	120°	720°
Heptagon	7	128.5°	900°
Octagon	8	135°	1080°

B. Students should notice that the measure of the interior angles increases with the number of sides. They may notice that the angle sum increases by 180° with each additional side, starting from the triangle.

Problem 4.1

Count the sides of each of these six regular polygons. Measure the interior angles with your angle ruler.

A. Make a table that shows the name of each polygon, the number of sides it has, the measure of each of its angles, and the sum of the measures of all of its angles (this is called the *angle sum*).

B. In your table, look for patterns that relate the number of sides a polygon has to the measure of its angles and to its angle sum. Think about ways to complete these statements:

- If a regular polygon has _____ sides, the angle sum of the polygon is _____ degrees.

- If a regular polygon has _____ sides, each angle measures _____ degrees.

▓ Problem 4.1 Follow-Up

The patterns you observed relating the number of sides of a regular polygon to the measures of its interior angles were based on measurements of one set of figures. Do you think the same patterns relating the number of sides and the sum of the angles will occur in larger or smaller regular polygons?

Below and on the next page are sets of regular polygons of different sizes. Measure the interior angles in each polygon to see whether the same side-angle patterns occur.

Answer to Problem 4.1 Follow-Up

Students should conclude that the length of the sides in the similar polygons has no effect on the angle sum or the measure of the interior angles.

Measuring Irregular Polygons

Launch

■ Propose the question of whether the side-angle patterns students discovered in their work with regular polygons will extend to irregular polygons.

Explore

■ Circulate as groups measure the polygons and look for side-angle patterns.

■ Correct any misuse of the angle ruler, and encourage students to label their drawings properly.

Summarize

■ As a class, share and analyze results until students see that the side-angle patterns hold for irregular polygons.

■ Have students prepare their findings for a class display. (*optional*)

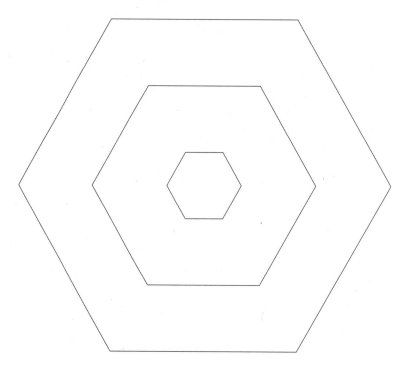

4.2 Measuring Irregular Polygons

In Problem 4.1, you discovered that the angle sum of any *regular* polygon can be predicted easily from the number of sides it has.

Regular polygon	Number of sides	Angle sum
Triangle	3	180°
Square	4	360°
Pentagon	5	540°
Hexagon	6	720°
Heptagon	7	900°
Octagon	8	1080°

In this problem, you will explore *irregular* polygons, like the ones shown below. An **irregular** polygon is a polygon in which the sides are not all the same length. Is there a relationship between the number of sides and the angle sum for irregular polygons?

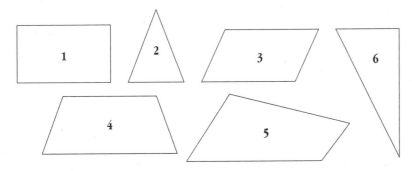

Problem 4.2

A. For each triangle and quadrilateral shown above, measure each interior angle and compute the angle sum.

B. How do the angle sums for these irregular polygons compare with the angle sums for the regular polygons?

C. Test the side-angle patterns you found by measuring the interior angles of some other triangles and quadrilaterals from your Shapes Set.

D. Use the information you have discovered about triangles and quadrilaterals to make a guess about the angle sums in irregular pentagons and hexagons. Test your guess by drawing and measuring some irregular pentagons and hexagons.

■ **Problem 4.2 Follow-Up**

Triangles with all sides equal are called **equilateral triangles.** Triangles with two sides equal, like shape 2 above, are called **isosceles triangles.** What can you say about the angles in an equilateral triangle? What can you say about the angles in an isosceles triangle?

Answers to Problem 4.2

A. The angle sum is 180° for each triangle and 360° for each quadrilateral.

B. The angle sums for irregular triangles and quadrilaterals are the same as for regular triangles and quadrilaterals.

C. Students should find similar results for all the triangles and quadrilaterals they measure.

D. The sum of the angle measures of an irregular pentagon is 540°. The sum of the angle measures of an irregular hexagon is 720°.

Answer to Problem 4.2 Follow-Up

In an equilateral triangle all the angles are equal, and since the sum of the angle measures

Back to the Bees!

At a Glance

Grouping: Small Groups

Launch

- Have students recall what they know about which regular polygons will tile.

- Pose the idea of using mathematics to determine whether a polygon can tile.

Explore

- Circulate as groups work with their polygons, and focus their attention on the role of angles in determining whether a polygon can tile.

- Have groups explore the same questions for the three irregular polygons.

- Have groups investigate combinations of polygons that they have already determined will tile. (*optional*)

Summarize

- As a class, share results.

The surface of a honeycomb is covered with hexagons. It seems reasonable that a honeycomb is covered with a simple shape instead of several complex shapes, but we obviously can't ask bees why their honeycomb construction results in hexagons instead of pentagons or heptagons or some other shape. However, there are some mathematical properties of hexagons that may offer explanations.

At right is a tiling of regular hexagons. Notice that three angles fit together exactly around each vertex point. Why do three regular hexagons fit together so neatly?

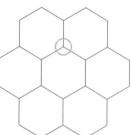

In Problem 1.1, you discovered which regular polygons fit together to cover a surface. In this problem, you will explore the properties of these shapes that allow them to fit together neatly around a vertex point.

Problem 4.3

Explore tilings made from a single type of regular polygon. Consider patterns with triangles only, squares only, pentagons only, hexagons only, heptagons only, and octagons only. Make sketches to show what you discover.

A. Which regular polygons fit around a vertex point exactly? What are the angle measures of these polygons?

B. Which regular polygons do not fit around a point exactly? What are the angle measures of these polygons?

C. What seems to be the key that tells which regular polygons will fit together in a tiling and which will not?

Problem 4.3 Follow-Up

Explore tilings made with parallelograms. Look for patterns in the angle measures of parallelograms that fit around a vertex point exactly. Make a record of your findings.

Assignment Choices

ACE question 4 and unassigned choices from earlier problems

Answers to Problem 4.3

A. Six triangles ($6 \times 60° = 360°$), four squares ($4 \times 90° = 360°$), and three hexagons ($3 \times 120° = 360°$) will fit around a vertex point.

B. Pentagons (interior angle = 108°), heptagons (128.5°), and octagons (135°) will not fit around a vertex point.

C. If their angle measures are factors of 360°, they will fit together.

Answer to Problem 4.3 Follow-Up

Any parallelogram will tile a surface, but students must be careful to match up sides of the same length.

Applications • Connections • Extensions

As you work on these ACE questions, use your calculator whenever you need it.

Applications

1. This figure is a regular decagon.

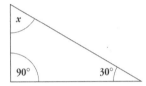

a. What angle sum do you expect for this polygon?

b. What measure do you expect for each interior angle of this polygon?

c. Can copies of this polygon be used to tile a surface? Explain your reasoning.

In 2–5, you are given measures of several angles. Find the measures of the other angles.

2.

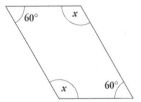

3.

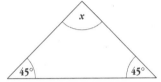

4.

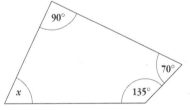

5.

Connections

6a. The diagonals divide the polygons into triangles. The angle sum of any triangle is 180°. So the angle sum of any polygon is the angle sum of the triangles formed by the sides and the diagonals drawn from one vertex.

6b. Because triangles are stable, you could increase the stability of other polygons by bracing them with interior triangles.

7a. Angles *ABC* and *CDA* have measure 121°. Angles *ABD* and *CDB* have measure 35°. Angles *DBC* and *BDA* have measure 86°. Angles *BCA* and *DAC* have measure 38°. Angles *BCD* and *DAB* have measure 59°. Angles *ACD* and *CAB* have measure 21°.

7b. Students will probably see that these four pairs of angles are equal: angles *ABD* and *CDB* (35°), angles *BDA* and *DBC* (86°), angles *CAB* and *ACD* (21°), and angles *DAC* and *BCA* (38°). These four pairs of angles represent one of the parallel line theorems in geometry: When two parallel lines are cut by a transversal, the alternate interior angles are congruent. These angles are alternate interior angles for pairs of parallel lines, and the diagonals are transversals. They will probably also see that opposite angles of the parallelogram—angles *ABC* and *ADC* (121°), and angles *DAB* and *BCD* (59°)—are equal.

Connections

6. Shown below are a quadrilateral and a pentagon with *diagonals* drawn to form triangles. A **diagonal** of a polygon is a segment connecting two vertices that are not next to each other.

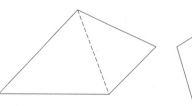 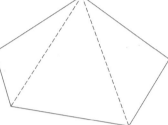

a. How do these drawings show a connection between angle sums of triangles, quadrilaterals, and pentagons?

b. What do the drawings show about ways to strengthen quadrilateral or pentagonal shapes in buildings?

7. In geometric figures, it is often useful to label points with letters. That way, you can describe any angle by using three letters. For example, the angle marked in the drawing below is angle DAC. In this notation, the middle letter is the vertex of the angle and the other two letters are points on each edge. To indicate that you are referring to an angle, you can write the word *angle* before the three letters (for example, angle DAC) or you can use an angle symbol (for example, ∠DAC).

a. Find and measure ∠ABC, ∠ABD, ∠DBC, ∠BCA, ∠BCD, ∠ACD, ∠CDB, ∠CDA, ∠BDA, ∠DAC, ∠DAB, and ∠CAB. Record your answers.

b. What relationships do you see among the angles in this figure?

8. Choose a nonrectangular quadrilateral (such as shape U) from your Shapes Set, or draw your own. Try to fit copies of your quadrilateral exactly around a point. Sketch a picture to help you explain what you found.

9. Choose a nonregular triangle (such as shape I) from your Shapes Set, or draw your own. Try to fit copies of your triangle exactly around a point. Sketch a picture to help explain what you found.

Extensions

10. a. Measure the interior angles of the star below and compare your results to the angle measures for the regular decagon.

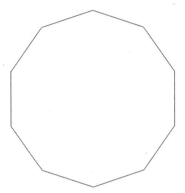

b. Draw other unusual polygons, and measure their interior angles to look for a pattern in the angle sums related to the number of sides.

11. Find all the line and turn symmetries for the star and the regular decagon above. How do the symmetries for the figures compare?

(**Teaching Tip:** You might need to emphasize the difference between the triangles formed in problem 6 and those formed in problem 7. You cannot use the sum of the angles in all four triangles to find the sum of the angles of quadrilateral *ABCD*.)

8. See page 50h.

9. See page 50h.

Extensions

10a. See page 50h.

10b. No matter how unusual the polygon looks, the sum of the angles will always be a multiple of 180°. If the polygon has *n* sides, the sum of the angles is (*n* − 2) × 180°.

11. See page 50i.

1a. In a regular polygon, the number of angles is the same as the number of sides. The measure of each angle is the same. A triangle has an angle sum of 180°. For each additional side, we add 180° to the angle sum. This means that a square has an angle sum of 360°, a pentagon has an angle sum of 540°, and so on. (Some students may see that this pattern is 180° times two less than the number of sides.) The number of degrees in an interior angle increases as the number of sides increases. We can find this measure by dividing the angle sum by the number of angles.

1b. The same pattern for the angle sum holds for irregular polygons. Any triangle has an angle sum of 180°, and 180° is added to the angle sum for each side added to the triangle. Generally, we cannot find the individual angles of an irregular polygon without measuring them.

2. For any tiling of polygons, the sum of the angles surrounding the vertex point must be 360°. This means that only regular polygons whose angle measure is a factor of 360° can form a tiling: the regular triangle, square, and hexagon.

Mathematical Reflections

In this investigation, you have explored patterns in the angle sums of regular and irregular polygons. You have looked at the relationship between the number of sides in a regular polygon and the size of its interior angles. And you have discovered how the angle measures of a polygon determine whether copies of it will fit exactly around a vertex point. These questions will help you summarize what you have learned:

1 **a.** In regular polygons, what patterns relate the number of sides to the angle sum and the size of the interior angles?

   b. In irregular polygons, what patterns relate the number of sides to the angle sum and the size of the interior angles?

2 How do these side-angle patterns explain why some polygons can tile the plane and others cannot?

Think about your answers to these questions, discuss your ideas with other students and your teacher, and then write a summary of your findings in your journal.

Are you noticing examples of tilings around you? Don't forget to write about them in your journal!

Tip for the Linguistically Diverse Classroom

Diagram Code The Diagram Code technique is described in detail in *Getting to Know Connected Mathematics*. Students use a minimal number of words with drawings or diagrams to respond to questions that require writing. Example: Question 2—A student might answer this question by drawing a square in a tiling pattern with each angle labeled 90° with the explanation *90° + 90° + 90° + 90° = 360°* underneath, perhaps with some emphasis on *360°*.

TEACHING THE INVESTIGATION

4.1 • Relating Sides to Angles

The goal of this problem is to have students measure interior angles in regular polygons, find the angle sums, form conjectures about a rule to predict what happens to the angle sum as the number of sides increases, and then refine their rule. Students should also be able to apply the rule in reverse—by knowing the measure of the angles in a regular polygon, they should be able to tell how many sides it has. Students also measure angles in nested polygons to develop the notion that the length of the sides in a regular polygon is irrelevant in relation to the side-angle patterns they observe.

Launch

The six shapes used in this problem are the same six that were used in Problem 1.1. Help make this connection for the students, reminding them of what makes a polygon a *regular* polygon.

> In Investigation 1, we experimented with the six regular polygons shown in your books on page 42. Someone remind us what a regular polygon is.

Take a few suggestions, and clarify them until the definition is correct.

> In Investigation 1, we were trying to find out which of these shapes would fit together nicely like tiles on a floor. We want to continue to think about these regular polygons by investigating the size of their angles and what happens to the measures of the interior angles as the number of sides increases.

> Which of the angles of these six regular polygons appears to be the smallest?

> Which of the angles of these six regular polygons appears to be the largest?

These questions are asking students to make informal observations about the sizes of the interior angles without using measuring tools. Don't move on until students are able to see that the size of the interior angles increases as the number of sides increases. One way to help struggling students see this is to demonstrate at the overhead projector how the sizes of the angles compare by placing one shape on top of another.

Once students understand this idea, turn them loose to work with a partner on Problem 4.1.

Explore

During this time, students should be recording their measurements so they can share their results later with the class. If a group is having trouble recording, have them look again at what part A is asking them to keep track of.

Summarize

Display a chart similar to the one below. With input from the class, fill in the missing information. Accept and record all answers on the chart.

Polygon	Number of sides	Interior angle	Angle sum
Triangle			
Square			
Pentagon			
Hexagon			
Heptagon			
Octagon			

Many students will have angle measures that are close to the actual measures but not exact. Some students may disagree with the measurements others give. One teacher handled this in the following manner:

> I have listed the names of the six regular polygons you had to measure. For the triangle, what numbers do you have to fill in the next three columns? Does anyone have anything different?

When a group answered yes, the teacher also recorded its numbers in the appropriate columns. For example, one group said the triangle has three sides and each interior angle measures 59°, for a total of 177°. Another group said that the triangle has three sides and each interior angle measures 60°, for a total of 180°. The teacher listed both of these groups' answers:

Polygon	Number of sides	Interior angle	Angle sum
Triangle	3	59°, 60°	177°, 180°

The teacher left both answers on the chart and continued to collect information on the remaining polygons. Once the chart was complete, she started to question what was on the chart.

> Why do we have different answers when we all measured the same angles? Does anyone have a suggestion for how we might resolve the angle measures we disagree on?

In this class, many students suggested remeasuring the interior angles. This resulted in some of the measures being eliminated from the chart. However, some students had given smaller angle measurements for pentagons than for squares.

> Look at all the answers that are now recorded on the chart. Are their any that don't seem reasonable?

Students argued for the elimination of some of the measures. The teacher only removed numbers from the chart when students had given a mathematical reason for eliminating them.

What patterns do you notice in the way the size of the interior angles is growing? What patterns do you notice in the way the size of the angle sum is growing?

Some students noticed that the angle sum seemed to be increasing by about 180° with each additional side. As a result, more numbers were eliminated from the chart because they did not fit the pattern. The teacher continued with the discussion until the class had arrived at the correct measurements.

Polygon	Number of sides	Interior angle	Angle sum
Triangle	3	60°	180°
Square	4	90°	360°
Pentagon	5	108°	540°
Hexagon	6	120°	720°
Heptagon	7	128.5°	900°
Octagon	8	135°	1080°

The teacher then tried to extend students' understanding by asking if-then statements:

If a regular polygon has nine sides, what will be the sum of all the angles in that polygon? Explain why your answer makes sense.

If a regular polygon has nine sides, each interior angle must be how many degrees? How did you arrive at that measure?

If a regular polygon has ten sides, what will be the sum of all the angles in that polygon? Explain your answer.

If a regular polygon had ten sides, each angle measure must be how many degrees? Explain your answer.

The class added this new information to the data chart:

Polygon	Number of sides	Interior angle	Angle sum
Nonagon	9	140°	1260°
Decagon	10	144°	1440°

If you gently encourage students to make observations about patterns in the chart, some may look at the angle sums and observe the relationship to the triangle's 180° angle sum. You may have a student who extends this relationship, noticing that the square contains two triangles (by drawing one diagonal, $180° \times 2 = 360°$), the pentagon contains three triangles (by drawing two diagonals from one vertex, $180° \times 3 = 540°$), and so on. However, if students are not prepared to make this kind of observation on their own, it is best not to force the issue. After all, the triangles made with diagonals are not equilateral triangles, and students have not yet worked with irregular triangles (which also have an angle sum of 180°).

Problem 4.1 Follow-Up tries to expand the ideas students have just developed. Students are asked to consider what happens to the angles of regular polygons when the length of the sides changes. They measure the angles of the nested polygons and observe that they remain the same regardless of the side length. The larger figure is *similar* to the smaller figure. In similar figures, interior angles are the same. (These ideas are developed more fully in the *Stretching and Shrinking* unit.)

For the Teacher: Triangulation

One way to reason about the angle sum in a polygon is to *triangulate* the polygon: start at any vertex, and draw all the possible diagonals from that vertex. Triangulating a square gives two triangles, triangulating a pentagon gives three triangles, triangulating a hexagon gives four triangles, and so on. Each time the number of sides increases by one, the number of triangles increases by one, making a pattern: 3 sides give 1 triangle, 4 sides give 2 triangles, 5 sides give 3 triangles, 6 sides give 4 triangles, and so on.

We can use symbols to state a rule for this pattern. If we let *n* represent the number of sides in a polygon, then (*n* – 2) represents the number of triangles we get by triangulating the polygon. If we multiply by 180° for each triangle, we have the formula:

(*n* – 2) × 180° = the angle sum in an *n*-sided polygon

Note that this is true for both regular and irregular polygons.

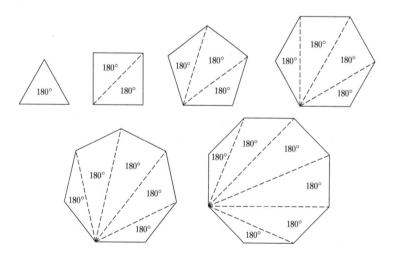

For a regular polygon, we can find the number of degrees in an interior angle by dividing the angle sum by the number of angles:

$$\frac{(n - 2) \times 180°}{n} = \text{the number of degrees in an angle of an } n\text{-sided regular polygon}$$

4.2 • Measuring Irregular Polygons

The exploration in this problem should lead students to the conclusion that all triangles have an angle sum of 180°, all quadrilaterals have an angle sum of 360°, and so on. They will discover this by measuring the angles in a variety of irregular triangles and quadrilaterals. They will use that information to make a conjecture about the angle sum in irregular pentagons and hexagons and to test their conjecture.

Launch

Introduce the idea of extending recent discoveries about regular polygons to irregular polygons.

> In the last problem, you discovered a relationship between the number of sides of a regular polygon and its angle sum. Today, we want to see if the pattern you discovered was simply the result of measuring regular polygons, or if the pattern will hold true for *irregular* polygons.

Explore

Students can measure the shapes shown in the student edition or use Labsheet 4.2, Irregular Polygons. As you walk around the room, question any student who has a measurement that is unreasonable.

> As I look at the angle and think about how it compares to a right angle, your measurement doesn't seem reasonable. Show me how you arrived at your measurement for that angle.

Watching students measure angles will help you to correct errors, such as moving the arm of the angle ruler in the wrong direction, working with the ruler upside down, and reading the unnumbered marks on the ruler incorrectly.

Continue to reinforce the practice that every angle should be labeled with its measure. Also ask students to label each figure with its angle sum. This will help you and members of the group to identify any measurement that is far from the desired 180° for triangles and 360° for quadrilaterals.

If students drew irregular triangles and quadrilaterals as homework, have them measure them in part C. When students draw irregular pentagons and hexagons in part D, encourage them to use straightedges and to make fairly large drawings, since the angles will be more distinct and easier to measure.

Summarize

After sharing and discussing the results from the different groups in the class, students should be able to generalize that all triangles have an angle sum of 180° and all quadrilaterals have an angle sum of 360°. Since these angle sums match the sums for regular polygons, most students will guess that the angle sum for any pentagon will be 540° and the angle sum for any hexagon will be 720°. Students should have drawn at least one of each of these shapes and found an angle sum very close to the expected sum.

If time permits, you might have groups prepare a display of their findings for the triangles, quadrilaterals, pentagons, or hexagons. The displays could show the shapes students worked with, the angle measures of the shapes, and the conclusions students made.

4.3 • **Back to the Bees!**

This problem extends the angle measuring done in Problems 4.1 and 4.2. Students examine the angle measures of polygons that fit together to form a tiling.

Launch

Remind students about the discussion that began in Investigation 1 about which shapes will tile a surface and which will not.

> Which of the regular polygon shapes we have (shapes A–F) did we learn would tile a surface—fit together so that there are no gaps or over-laps—by themselves?

Students should recall that the triangle, square, and hexagon all fit that requirement.

Have students recall the shape of the polygon that covers the surface of a honeycomb. Focus their attention on the vertex points of the hexagon tiling on page 46 of the student edition.

> How could we tell for sure that a shape, like these hexagons, fits exactly around each vertex point in a tiling? We know the fit looks good, but how can we use mathematics to tell for sure?

Have students work in groups to explore the questions posed in Problem 4.3.

Explore

As you move from group to group, ask questions about angles to help students focus on them as a consideration in forming a tiling.

> What amount of turn must we have to completely surround a vertex point? How many degrees are in the angles of the polygon you are investigating? How many degrees are in all of the angles around this vertex point? What would we expect the angle sum around a vertex to be?

If a group is having trouble getting started, you might suggest that they draw a dot on a piece of paper and then try to surround the dot—the vertex point—with angles of the polygon with which they are working.

Remind students to record what they find, using sketches and recording angle measurements to help show why their answers make sense.

When students have completed the exploration of the regular polygons, they should move to the follow-up and work with parallelograms.

If you have time and your students seem interested, pose an additional challenge. Ask students to figure out why the combinations of shapes they found for Problem 1.1 will tile by investigating their angle measurements. Be sure to ask them to show why they think their design forms a tiling with no gaps or overlaps. One simple example is octagons and squares: the interior angle in a regular octagon is 135°, two octagons would be 270°, and adding an angle from the square would make the necessary 360°.

Summarize

Students should be prepared to discuss their findings. Of the regular polygons, the triangle, the square, and the hexagon can be laid down in a tiling pattern; the pentagon, heptagon, and octagon cannot.

For the Teacher: Revisiting ACE Question 13

ACE question 13 in Investigation 1 relates to the ideas discussed in this investigation. Revisiting this problem may help more students make sense of it now because of their work in this unit.

Focus students' attention on a vertex point in a tiling such as the one below. There is exactly one copy of each of the angles of the quadrilateral around a vertex point, so the sum of the angles of the quadrilateral must be 360°.

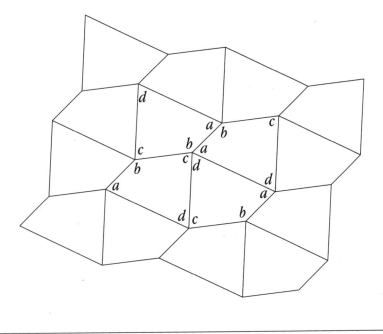

Additional Answers

ACE Answers

Connections

8. Students should be able to come up with four copies of their quadrilateral surrounding a vertex point, with different angles of the quadrilateral touching the vertex point.

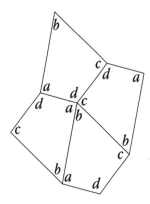

9. Students should be able to come up with six copies of their triangle surrounding a vertex point. Two copies of each angle should surround the vertex point.

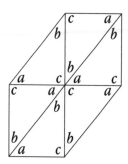

Extensions

10a. The interior angles alternate between 36° at the points of the star and 252° between the points of the star. We can add the five 36° angles (180°) to the five 252° angles (1260°) for a total of 1440°. The regular decagon has the same angle sum, 1440°.

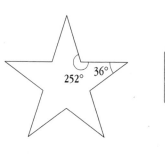

11. The star has five line symmetries: the lines from each small interior angle to the opposite larger interior angle.

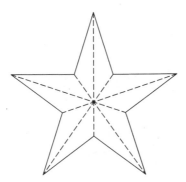

The star also has five turn symmetries since any of the five points can be turned onto the former position of any other point. Since 360° ÷ 5 = 72°, the turn symmetries are 72°, 144°, 216°, 288°, and 360°.

The decagon has ten line symmetries: five as in the star, joining opposite vertices, plus five more connecting the midpoints of opposite edges.

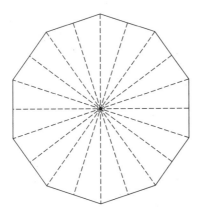

The decagon has ten turn symmetries, since you can turn it so that any vertex lies in the former position of any other vertex. Since there are ten vertices, every multiple of 360° ÷ 10, or 36°, is a turn symmetry.

For the Teacher: Finding Polygon Diagonals

Your more curious students may enjoy exploring the number of diagonals that can be drawn in a polygon. If you consider a polygon with n vertices, you can draw $(n - 3)$ diagonals from each vertex—since you cannot draw a diagonal from the vertex to itself or to either of the adjacent vertices. When you have counted all the possible diagonals in this way, you have counted each one twice (once from each end). So, the total number of diagonals in a polygon with n vertices is $\dfrac{n(n - 3)}{2}$.

Side-Angle-Shape Connections

In this investigation, we focus on the properties of sides and angles of equilateral and isosceles triangles, squares, rectangles, and parallelograms. Because of symmetry, you can remove a shape from a tiling of one of these polygons, flip or turn it in various ways, and fit it back into the same space. In Problems 5.1 and 5.2, students describe ways to flip or turn each of these shapes to put it in orientations that will fit back in the space in the tiling. In their exploration, students will discover the properties of shapes that determine which flips and turns are possible.

Mathematical and Problem-Solving Goals

- ■ *To recognize and describe flips and turns that will return a triangle, square, rectangle, or parallelogram to its original orientation*

- ■ *To understand the properties of sides and angles in isosceles and equilateral triangles, squares, rectangles, and parallelograms*

Materials		
Problem	For students	For the teacher
All	Calculators, ShapeSet (1 per group)	Transparencies 5.1 and 5.2 (optional), Shapes A, B, J, M, and P from the ShapeSet for use on the overhead projector (optional; copy the blackline masters onto transparency film.)

Student Pages 51–63   Teaching the Investigation 63a–63f

Side-Angle-Shape Connections

In your study of the sides, angles, and shapes of polygons, you have discovered some important facts of geometry. For example, if you want to build a rectangle, you know that you need to make opposite sides the same length and all angles 90°.

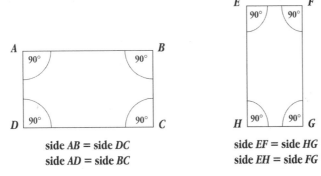

side *AB* = side *DC*
side *AD* = side *BC*

side *EF* = side *HG*
side *EH* = side *FG*

Knowing these properties of rectangles helps people to use rectangles to make designs and to construct buildings. Many other relationships among the sides and angles of polygons are useful properties.

Think about this!

What properties have you noticed about the sides and angles in triangles, quadrilaterals, pentagons, hexagons, and octagons? Consider relationships such as those found in the lengths of sides, measures of angles, or angle sums.

5.1

Flipping and Turning Triangles

Launch

- In a class discussion, demonstrate the meanings of *flip* and *turn*, and help students to be precise when describing flips and turns.

- Demonstrate how to record flips and turns.

Explore

- As students work, help them keep track of vertices and record their findings.

- Have students move on to Problem 5.2. (*optional*)

Summarize

- Have students share their findings in a class discussion. If students work on Problems 5.1 and 5.2 on the same day, summarize the problems together.

Assignment Choices

Unassigned choices from earlier problems

5.1 **Flipping and Turning Triangles**

The first pattern below is made with *equilateral triangles*. In an **equilateral triangle**, all three sides are the same length. The second pattern is made with *isosceles triangles*. In an **isosceles triangle**, two sides are the same length.

There is one piece missing from each pattern. To the left of each pattern is a triangle that will fit in the hole. The vertices of these triangles are numbered.

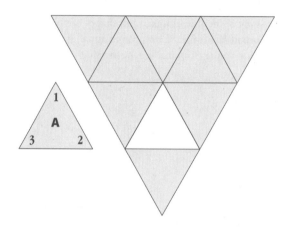

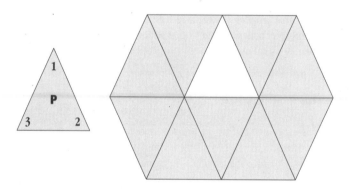

We can flip or turn the triangle so that it will fit into the space in the tiling. *Flipping* a shape means turning it over, like this:

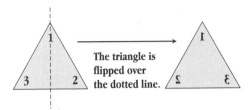

The triangle is flipped over the dotted line.

Turning a shape means rotating it, like this:

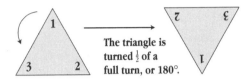

The triangle is turned ½ of a full turn, or 180°.

There are many ways to flip and turn a shape.

Problem 5.1

A. In the tiling of equilateral triangles, describe all the different ways the shape can be placed in the hole. How many ways are there in all?

B. In the tiling of isosceles triangles, describe all the different ways the shape can be placed in the hole. Is the number of ways you can put the isosceles triangle in the hole less than, greater than, or equal to the number of ways you can put the equilateral triangle in the hole? Explain.

You may find it helpful to use your Shapes Set to investigate the different ways you can flip and turn the triangle. Use the numbers on the vertices of the triangles to help you describe how each triangle can be flipped and turned to position it in the hole in different ways.

▨ Problem 5.1 Follow-Up

1. What do your answers indicate about relations between sides and angles in equilateral triangles?

2. What do your answers indicate about relations between sides and angles in isosceles triangles?

Answers to Problem 5.1

See page 63d.

Answers to Problem 5.1 Follow-Up

1. The equilateral triangle can be rotated so any angle of the triangle matches with any angle of the hole and any side of the triangle matches with any side of the hole. This means that all the angles are equal and all the sides are equal.

2. The isosceles triangle can be flipped over the line from the vertex between the two equal sides (vertex 1) to the midpoint of the opposite side. This means that the angles opposite the equal sides—angles 2 and 3—are equal.

Flipping and Turning Quadrilaterals

At a Glance

Grouping:
Small Groups

Launch

■ If Problem 5.2 is explored on a different day from Problem 5.1, refocus students on the question and review how to record findings.

Explore

■ As students work, help them keep track of vertices and record their findings.

Summarize

■ Have students share their findings in a class discussion.

■ Discuss the fact that the equilateral triangle and the square have the same number of lines of symmetry as they have sides, and (*optional*) extend the discussion to all regular polygons.

5.2 **Flipping and Turning Quadrilaterals**

The three tilings below and on the next two pages are made of squares, of rectangles, and of parallelograms. Again, one piece is missing from each pattern.

> ### Problem 5.2
>
> **A.** In the tiling of squares, describe all the different ways the shape can be placed in the hole. How many ways are there in all?
>
> **B.** In the tiling of rectangles, describe all the different ways the shape can be placed in the hole. How many ways are there in all?
>
> **C.** In the tiling of parallelograms, describe all the different ways the shape can be placed in the hole. How many ways are there in all?
>
> You may find it helpful to use your Shapes Set to investigate the different ways you can flip and turn the shapes. Use the numbers on the vertices of the shapes to help you describe how each shape can be flipped and turned to position it in the hole in different ways.

■ **Problem 5.2 Follow-Up**

1. What do your answers indicate about relations between sides and angles in squares?
2. What do your answers indicate about relations between sides and angles in rectangles?
3. What do your answers indicate about relations between sides and angles in parallelograms?

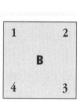

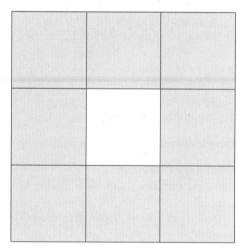

Assignment Choices

ACE questions 1–17, and unassigned choices from earlier problems

Assessment

It is appropriate to use Check-Up 2 after this problem.

Answers to Problem 5.2

See page 63e.

Answers to Problem 5.2 Follow-Up

See page 63f.

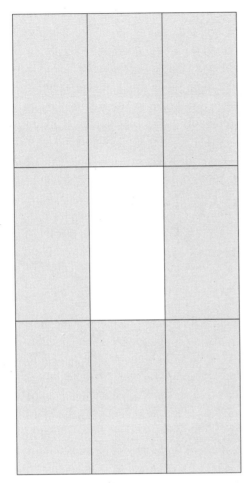

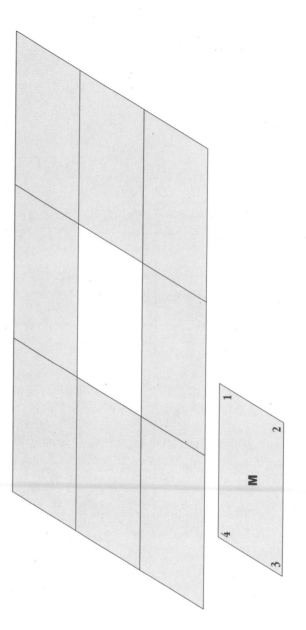

As you work on these ACE questions, use your calculator whenever you need it.

Applications

1. This map shows streets of Rectangle City, in which all city blocks are identical rectangles. Two side measurements are given.

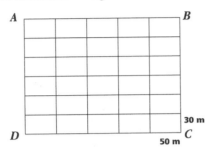

A   B

30 m

D   C

50 m

a. Find the shortest path from point *A* to point *C* along city streets. Explain how you know you have found the shortest path.

b. Find the shortest path from point *B* to point *D* along city streets. Explain how you know you have found the shortest path.

c. If you flew in a helicopter, you would not need to follow city blocks. Then which trip would be shorter—*A* to *C* or *B* to *D*?

2. This map shows streets of Parallelogram City, in which all city blocks are identical parallelograms. Two side measurements are given.

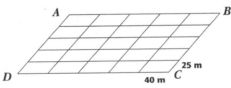

A   B

25 m

D   C

40 m

a. Find the shortest path from point *A* to point *C* along city streets. Explain how you know you have found the shortest path.

Answers

Applications

1a. There are many possible shortest paths from *A* to *C*, all of length 430 meters. Any path that moves down or to the right at each intersection will be a minimum-length path, and any minimum-length path from *A* to *C* must include six blocks down and five blocks across. (The number of minimal paths is related to the theory of Pascal's triangle, which will be explored in the *What Do You Expect?* unit.)

1b. The shortest paths from *B* to *D* will also be 430 meters because of the symmetry of the rectangles.

1c. The flight from *A* to *C* and from *B* to *D* will be the same length because of the symmetry of the rectangles. (The Pythagorean Theorem will be investigated in the *Oskars, Pythagoras, and Plimpton* unit.)

2a. The shortest path from *A* to *C* along city streets is 325 meters. Any path that moves diagonally down or to the right at each intersection will be a minimum-length path, and any minimum-length path from *A* to *C* must include five blocks down and five blocks across.

2b. The shortest path from *B* to *D* is also 325 meters, because opposite sides of a parallelogram are the same length.

2c. The flight from *A* to *C* is shorter than the flight from *B* to *D*, because the diagonals of these parallelograms are not the same length (in contrast to the diagonals of rectangles).

3. See page 63f.

4a. If we infer measurements of unlabeled segments from the principle that opposite sides of a rectangle are equal, the outside dimensions of the lot are 36 meters by 18 meters.

4b. 108 meters (This question is foreshadowing future work with perimeter. We do not recommend making any formal statement of a perimeter formula at this point.)

b. Find the shortest path from point *B* to point *D* along city streets. Explain how you know you have found the shortest path.

c. If you flew in a helicopter, you would not need to follow city blocks. Then which trip would be shorter—*A* to *C* or *B* to *D*?

3. Look at the angles formed by street corners in the map of Parallelogram City in question 2.

  a. Draw one of the blocks, and mark any angles that are the same size.

  b. Why do the sides of the blocks line up to give straight streets?

4. Below are the plans for a parking lot. The parking spaces are identical rectangles.

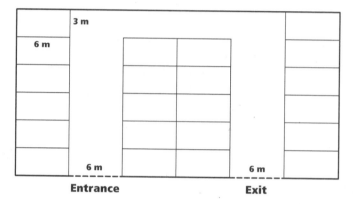

  a. What are the outside dimensions of the lot?

  b. How far would you have to walk to walk completely around the outside of the lot? Explain your reasoning.

Connections

5. Think back to the question posed at the start of this unit: Why are nearly all windows and doors in homes, schools, stores, and office buildings in the shape of rectangles (not triangles, circles, or trapezoids)? What have you learned in this unit that will help you to answer this question?

6. Below are three sets of identical quadrilaterals arranged around a point. What does the exact fit in each case show about the angle measures of the quadrilaterals?

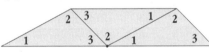

7. a. The illustrations below show what happened when three copies of a paper triangle were put together with the three different vertices of the triangle touching a single point and the sides of the same length matched up. Repeat this process for two different triangles that you design. Tape your results together and onto your answer paper.

b. What do your figures show about the sum of the measures of the angles in a triangle?

c. What other figures do you see in the arrangement of your three triangles?

d. What properties of angles do you see demonstrated in the arrangement of your three triangles?

Connections

5. Answers will vary. Students' explanations may include discussion of symmetries, parallel sides, or right angles. They may mention that it is probably easier to design a system for opening and closing rectangular doors and windows than doors and windows of other shapes.

6. In each of these sets of quadrilaterals, the four angles surrounding the point equal 360°. In the rectangle, all of the angles are equal.

7a. Pictures will vary. Each set of three triangles should show one of each vertex of the triangle touching a single point.

7b. Possible answer: The pictures show that angle 1 + angle 2 + angle 3 = 180° for any triangle. (180° is half of a full turn, and a 180° angle is a *straight angle.*)

7c. Possible answer: If you take away one of the lines inside the tiling, you see a parallelogram. If you take away both of the lines inside the tiling, you see a trapezoid.

7d. The three triangles make a trapezoid because it looks like the top is parallel to the base. The base is a straight line because the sum of the angles is 180°.

8. See below right.

9. See below right.

10. See page 63f.

11. See page 63f.

12. Possible answer:
(0, 0), (5, 0), (0, 3), (5, 3)

13. Possible answer:
(0, 0), (5, 0), (1, 3), (6, 3)

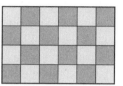

At the Sleepy Hollow Pottery Shop, artists use square tiles to make tabletops with colorful designs. They arrange the tiles in a rectangular pattern and then bend a metal strip to form a border. One simple design is shown here.

In 8–11, give the dimensions of every possible rectangle tabletop that could be made with the given number of tiles. For each possibility, find the length of the metal strip needed, and explain how it should be bent to make the border. You might find it helpful to use grid paper to draw and label the figures.

8. 128 tiles

9. 60 tiles

10. 35 tiles

11. 37 tiles

In 12–16, use a coordinate grid, like the one shown below.

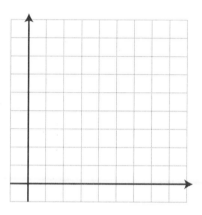

12. Give coordinates of four points that are vertices of a rectangle.

13. Give coordinates of four points that are vertices of a parallelogram that is *not* a rectangle.

8.

Table dimensions	Strip length	Possible bending points
1 × 128	258	1, 129, 130
2 × 64	132	2, 66, 68
4 × 32	72	4, 36, 40
8 × 16	48	8, 24, 32

9.

Table dimensions	Strip length	Possible bending points
1 × 60	122	1, 61, 62
2 × 30	64	2, 32, 34
3 × 20	46	3, 23, 26
4 × 15	38	4, 19, 23
5 × 12	34	5, 17, 22
6 × 10	32	6, 16, 22

14. If (0, 0) and (4, 6) are two vertices of a rectangle, what might be the coordinates of the other two vertices?

15. If (0, 0) and (1, 4) are two vertices of a parallelogram, what might be the coordinates of the other two vertices?

16. If (5, 0) and (6, 3) are two vertices of a parallelogram, what might be the coordinates of the other two vertices?

Extensions

17. Standard-size bricks are rectangular blocks that are approximately 5 cm by 10 cm by 20 cm. These bricks are often used like tiles to cover a sidewalk or the walls of a building.

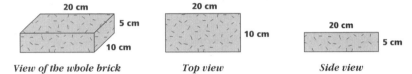

View of the whole brick   *Top view*   *Side view*

a. Draw several different patterns you could make with standard bricks.

b. If you look at the face of a brick wall, you usually see the pattern on the left below, not the simpler pattern on the right. Can you think of any reasons why bricklayers prefer the less simple pattern? (You might test your ideas by building a wall with blocks or dominoes.)

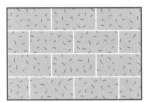   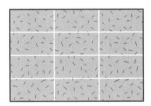

14. Possible answer: (4, 0), (0, 6)

15. Possible answer: (1, 1), (0, 3)

16. Possible answer: (0, 4), (1, 7)

Extensions

17a. See below left.

17b. Possible answer: In the overlapping pattern, cracks, once they have started, cannot run along the wall so easily.

17a. This question on brick patterns is something students can investigate either by simply looking at the buildings around them or by doing some research in books on architecture and design. There are lots of different bricklaying patterns in patios and sidewalks. Possible answers:

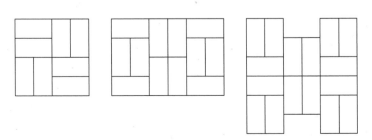

18. See below right.

19. See below right.

20a. Possible answer: If you drew a straight line from *B* to the bottom, then moved the triangle over to the left-hand side of the remaining figure, it would make a rectangle.

20b. Possible answer: This shows that angle *C* and angle *D* add to 180°. (They are supplementary.)

In 18 and 19, refer to this map of Rectangle City:

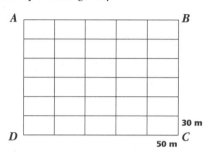

18. Find the longest possible path from point *A* to point *C*, walking along city streets but not covering any block side twice.

19. Find the longest possible path from point *A* to point *D*, walking along city streets but not covering any block side twice.

20. a. How could the parallelogram below be cut into two pieces and put back together to make a rectangle?

   b. What does your answer show about the relations among angles of a parallelogram?

18. We found a path that is 2450 meters long:

19. We found a path that is 2400 meters long:

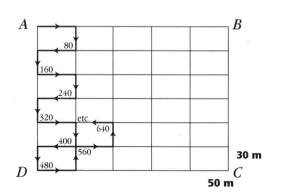
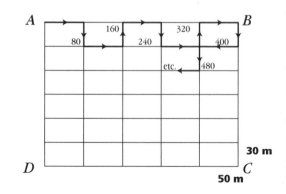

Mathematical Reflections

In this investigation, you have explored side-angle relationships for triangles and quadrilaterals. These questions will help you summarize what you have learned:

1. What is true about the lengths of the sides and the measures of the angles in a triangle with three equal angles?

2. What is true about the lengths of the sides and the measures of the angles in a triangle with two equal angles?

3. What is true about the lengths of the sides and the measures of the angles in a square?

4. What is true about the lengths of the sides and the measures of the angles in a rectangle that is not a square?

5. What is true about the lengths of the sides and the measures of the angles in a parallelogram that is not a rectangle?

Think about your answers to these questions, discuss your ideas with other students and your teacher, and then write a summary of your findings in your journal.

What side-angle-shape connections have you noticed in the world around you? You may want to include drawings to help you communicate what you have discovered about side-angle-shape connections.

Possible Answers

1. All sides must be equal and all angles must be 60°.

2. The sides opposite the two equal angles must be equal. The sum of the angles is 180°.

3. All the sides are the same length. All the angles are 90°.

4. Opposite sides are the same length, but all the sides are not equal. All the angles are 90°.

5. Opposite sides are the same length. The sum of the angles is 360°.

Questions 1 and 2 are based on the fact that if any two sides in a triangle are equal, the angles opposite those sides are equal. In questions 3, 4, and 5, students should recognize that four-sided figures cannot be determined by the lengths of their sides alone. The angles in 3 and 4 must be right angles; in 5 the angles must *not* be right angles. In 3 all sides must be equal; in 4 and 5 opposite sides must be equal; in 4 all sides *cannot* be equal.

Tip for the Linguistically Diverse Classroom

Original Rebus The Original Rebus technique is described in detail in *Getting to Know Connected Mathematics*. Students make a copy of the text before it is discussed. During discussion, they generate their own rebuses for words they do not understand as the words are made comprehensible through pictures, objects, or demonstrations Example: Item 1—key words for which students may make rebuses are *true, lengths, sides, triangle,* and *angles.*

5.1 • Flipping and Turning Triangles

In Problem 5.1, students determine how many different ways isosceles and equilateral triangles can be reoriented and then returned to a space in a tiling. They describe how to achieve each orientation by means of a flip or a turn. In the process of experimenting, students are asked to think about what symmetries the shapes have and how symmetry is related to the sides and angles of the shapes.

Launch

Problem 5.2 is a similar activity involving quadrilaterals. If possible, have students do Problems 5.1 and 5.2 on the same day. This launch is a sufficient introduction to both.

To launch the problem, help students become familiar with the situation. Have them take out shapes A and P and refer to the tiling of equilateral triangles on page 52 of the student edition. As students work at their desks, demonstrate at the overhead projector.

> Lay your equilateral triangle over the empty space in the drawing of shape A so the vertices are in the same position as they are in the drawing. Now, can you find a way to turn or flip your triangle so it will again fit exactly into the space?

Allow students to share their ideas. This will give you an opportunity to raise the issue of how to record a move so someone else can reproduce it. The following dialog occurred in one class.

Teacher: Can you explain exactly how you flipped or turned your triangle so that it fit back into the space? Try to explain it so we can reproduce what you did.

Karen: I just turned it over and put in into the missing space.

The teacher followed Karen's instructions. She flipped the triangle over a line through the midpoints of edge 1–2 and edge 1–3:

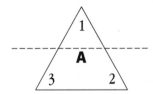 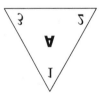

Teacher: My tile doesn't fit back in the hole. Can someone help us out?

Rashida: How about flipping the triangle over the line through the top point?

In response to such a suggestion, the teacher can challenge the suggestion either by following the student's instructions word for word, or by calling on a student who understands why the first student's language is not precise enough. This teacher followed the student's directions by flipping the triangle over the edge 1–3 (a line that goes "through the top point"), which again put the triangle in the wrong orientation:

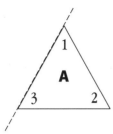 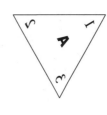

Teacher: It looks like you still need to be more precise. You need to describe exactly which line you want to flip the triangle over. You can describe a line by giving a couple of points on the line. And it helps to call a vertex by its number so we know exactly which vertex you are talking about.

Nathan: O.K. Let's flip the triangle over a line through vertex 1 and the center of the triangle.

Teacher: What do you mean by the "center" of the triangle?

Nathan: You know! The middle!

Teacher: Would we all find the same "middle" for every triangle? Can you describe another point on the line that you mean?

Nathan: Yeah. The center of the side 3–2.

Teacher: Mathematicians call the center of a side the *midpoint* of the side. Can you use this idea to describe your move?

Nathan: Flip the triangle over the line through vertex 1 and the midpoint of side 3–2.

The teacher demonstrated this flip:

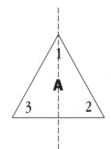 

The students realized that this flip did result in a correct orientation.

For the Teacher: Finding the Center of a Triangle

The line from the vertex of a triangle to the midpoint of the opposite side is called a *median line*. The intersection of the three median lines can be used to locate the point called the *center* or *centroid* of the triangle. The center is the balance point for a triangle. If you place the center of a triangle on a sharp point, it will balance.

You will want to have students suggest *turns* they think will work as well. Again, encourage them to be precise in telling exactly how much to turn the figure.

You might want to ask students how much of a complete turn is needed and then work on deciding what part of 360° this is. Your students might try to describe turns by telling you, for example, to turn vertex 1 onto vertex 2. This works, but it is mathematically imprecise. Describing this as a turn of 120°—which is $\frac{1}{3}$ of a complete turn—is more accurate.

When you feel the class understands how to record their work, let them work in pairs or small groups on the problem.

Explore

As you work with individual students or groups, you may need to help students describe the mirror lines and give the degree measures for the turn symmetries. Some will need to copy the vertex labels onto the back of the triangle; others will be comfortable just turning the triangle over to read the vertex labels. When students complete the problem have them move to Problem 5.1 Follow-Up.

Most students will be able to move right from Problem 5.1 to Problem 5.2. You will not need to launch Problem 5.2 separately.

Summarize

You will probably want to summarize Problems 5.1 and 5.2 together. Have students share their solutions in a class discussion. You may wish to have one student describe flips and turns while you or another student tries to reproduce them at the overhead projector.

5.2 • Flipping and Turning Quadrilaterals

Although this problem is a continuation of Problem 5.1, you may want to review that material if both problems are not discussed the same day.

Launch

You probably do not need to launch Problem 5.2 separately from Problem 5.1. However, if you assign the problems on different days, you may need to refocus students on the question and give them some reminders about how to record responses.

Explore

Have students work in pairs or small groups on the problem and the follow-up. Students may find it easier to turn their books sideways (so the shape's letter is right-side-up) to work with the tilings of rectangles and parallelograms. As you circulate, you may need to help students record their findings.

Summarize

Have students share their solutions (you will probably want to summarize Problems 5.1 and 5.2 together). You may wish to have one student describe flips and turns while you or another student tries to reproduce them at the overhead projector.

Point out that the equilateral triangle and the square (the only regular polygons tested) have as many lines of symmetry as they have sides. This is because all their sides and all their angles are equal.

You might want to challenge students to consider whether all regular polygons have as many lines of symmetry as they have sides. (This turns out to be true. For even-sided regular polygons, the lines of symmetry connect opposite vertices and opposite midpoints of sides, as in the square. In odd-sided regular polygons, the lines of symmetry connect vertices with the midpoints of the opposite side, as in the equilateral triangle.)

Discuss the fact that, if none of the sides of a polygon are the same length, there cannot be any lines of reflection or any turns other than the 360° turn. The shape will fit in a tiling in only one way.

Additional Answers

Answers to Problem 5.1

A. There are six ways to orient the triangle so that it fits into the hole:

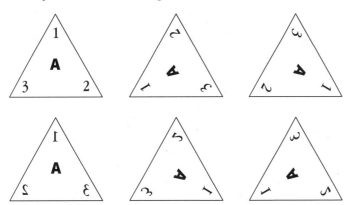

Possible way to arrive at these six orientations: The triangle can be turned 120°, 240°, or 360°, and it can be flipped over any of the three lines through a vertex and the midpoint of its opposite side.

B. There are two ways to orient the triangle so that it fits into the hole:

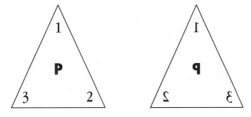

Possible way to arrive at these two orientations: The triangle can be rotated 360° and it can be flipped about the line from vertex 1 to the midpoint of the opposite side. There are fewer ways to put the isosceles triangle into the hole than there are to put the equilateral triangle into the hole. For an orientation to work, equal sides and equal angles must be matched up. An isosceles triangle has two equal sides and two equal angles so there are fewer ways to match up equal sides and equal angles than there are for an equilateral triangle, which has three equal sides and three equal angles.

Answers to Problem 5.2

A. There are eight ways to orient the square so that it fits into the hole:

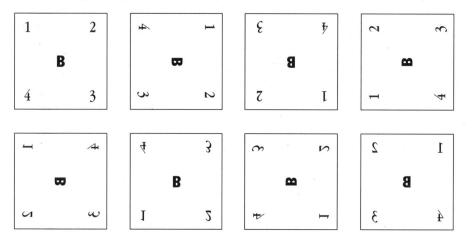

Possible way to arrive at these eight orientations: The square can be rotated 90°, 180°, 270°, or 360°; it can be flipped over each of the two diagonals; and it can be flipped over each of the two lines joining the midpoints of opposite sides.

B. There are four ways to orient the rectangle so that it fits into the hole:

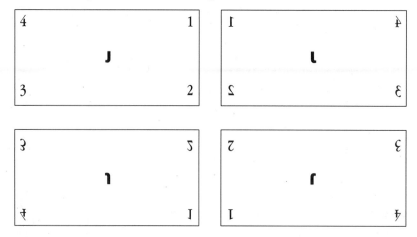

Possible way to arrive at these four orientations: The rectangle can be rotated 180° or 360°, and it can be flipped over each of the two lines joining the midpoints of opposite sides.

C. There are two ways to orient the parallelogram so that it fits into the hole:

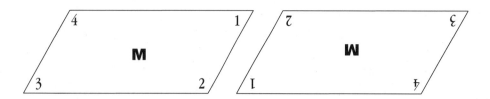

Possible way to arrive at these two orientations: The parallelogram can be rotated 180° or 360°.

Answers to Problem 5.2 Follow-Up

1. The square can be rotated so any angle matches with any angle of the hole and any side matches with any side of the hole. This indicates that all the sides are equal and all the angles are equal.

2. Rotating the rectangle 180° matches each side of the rectangle with its opposite side. This indicates that opposite sides are equal. The rotation also matches each angle with the angle diagonally across from it, so opposite angles must be equal. The flips match opposite sides also, but this time match adjacent angles, so adjacent angles must be equal.

3. Rotating the parallelogram 180° matches each side of the parallelogram with its opposite side. This indicates that opposite sides are equal. The rotation also matches each angle with the angle diagonally across from it, so opposite angles must be equal.

ACE Answers

Applications

3a. Opposite angles are equal:

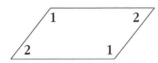

3b. Possible answer: Because the sum of the small angle and the large angle that fit together is 180°, and 180° is a straight angle

---

For the Teacher: Supplementary Angles

The sides of the blocks line up because in a parallelogram consecutive (not opposite) angles are supplementary (this wording is not introduced in the student edition and should probably not be used unless students seem to want a name for the condition in which two angles add to a straight line). Supplementary angles add to 180°.

Connections

10.	Table dimensions	Strip length	Possible bending points
	1 × 35	72	1, 36, 37
	5 × 7	24	5, 12, 17

11.	Table dimensions	Strip length	Possible bending points
	1 × 37	76	1, 38, 39

Turtle Tracks

This investigation engages students in computer activities that reinforce many of the ideas developed in previous investigations. The problems were written to be implemented on a Macintosh computer using an enhanced dialect of Logo called *Turtle Math*. However, they can easily be adapted to other Logo software packages running on either Macintosh or IBM-compatible computers.

Although these problems will ideally be done with two to four students per computer, we encourage you to do this investigation even if you have only a single demonstration computer.

In Problem 6.1, students use Logo commands to make designs. If your students do not have access to computers, they can do this problem with pencil and paper. In Problem 6.2, students write and debug programs for drawing triangles. If you have only a demonstration computer, you can do this problem as a class activity. Problem 6.3 reinforces ideas students have learned in earlier investigations by asking them to write Logo programs to make quadrilaterals. This problem can also be done with pencil and paper. Mastery of Logo is not a goal of this investigation!

Students usually enjoy these computer activities, and it may be tempting to spend a lot of time on this investigation. However, we recommend that you do not spend more than five days on these activities.

Mathematical and Problem-Solving Goals

- **To use a computer programming language to reinforce ideas about the properties of polygons**

- **To lay a foundation for students to visualize exterior angles**

	Materials	
Problem	**For students**	**For the teacher**
All	Calculators, Macintosh computers (optional; per 2-4 students), *Turtle Math* software (optional), grid paper (optional; provided as a blackline master)	Transparencies 6.1 to 6.3, Macintosh computer, preferably with a large-screen display (the problems can easily be adapted for other Logo software running on either Macintosh or IBM-compatibles); *Turtle Math* software (or other Logo software) **Note:** To run *Turtle Math*, a Macintosh must be model LC or better with 4 MB of RAM and System 7 or higher.

INVESTIGATION

Turtle Tracks

For thousands of years, the designs on houses, clothing, dishes, and tools were painted, woven, molded, and carved by human hands.

Calendar from ancient Crete

Reed basket made by Seri Indians of Northern Mexico

Over the past 300 years, machines have been invented to help with these tasks. In the past 50 years, factories have been automated. Most machines are now run by electric motors and controlled by computers. But the machines are only as smart as the human beings who plan the operations and program the computers. The programs for computer-controlled machines are written in mathematical languages in which measures of length and angles are used to tell machines what to do and robot tools how to move.

You can use a computer language called *Logo* to write instructions for drawing lines on a computer screen. In Logo, you type commands that tell a "turtle" how to move around the screen. As it moves, the turtle's path is shown on the screen. You can create designs by telling the turtle how to move.

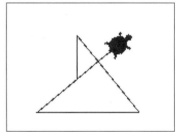

Tip for the Linguistically Diverse Classroom

Visual Enhancement The Visual Enhancement technique is described in detail in *Getting to Know Connected Mathematics*. It involves using real objects or pictures to make information comprehensible. Example: While discussing this page, you might show real objects or pictures of clothing, pottery, or other items that are painted or decorated by hand.

The turtle understands many different instructions, but you can make interesting designs by using just a few simple commands.

Greta wrote a set of Logo commands to draw her first initial. After typing each command, she pressed the **return** key to see the turtle move.

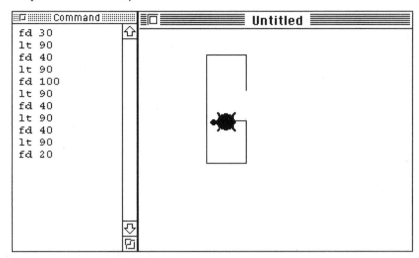

The commands that Greta used are from this list of common Logo commands. You can do all the problems in this investigation using only these eight commands. You can type the commands in capital letters or lowercase letters.

Common Logo Commands

fd   The *forward* command tells the turtle to move forward. The fd command must be followed by a space and a number telling the turtle how many steps to take. For example, fd 60 tells the turtle to move forward 60 steps.

bk   The *backward* command tells the turtle to move backward. The bk command must be followed by a space and a number telling the turtle how many steps to take. For example, bk 35 tells the turtle to move backward 35 steps.

Drawing with Logo

At a Glance

Grouping:
Small Groups

Launch

- At the demonstration computer, introduce students to the Free Explore screen and the four basic turtle commands.

- Show students how to edit commands in the Command window.

Explore

- Allow groups to explore making designs using Logo commands.

- Have students invent a game using Logo. (*optional*)

Summarize

- Allow each group to demonstrate one of their designs, or (if you have only a demonstration computer) edit the groups' designs as a class.

Assignment Choices

ACE questions 1–8 and unassigned choices from earlier problems

---

lt The *left turn* command tells the turtle to turn to its left. The lt command must be followed by a space and a number telling the turtle how many degrees to turn. For example, lt 30 tells the turtle to turn 30° to its left.

rt The *right turn* command tells the turtle to turn to its right. The rt command must be followed by a space and a number telling the turtle how many degrees to turn. For example, rt 45 tells the turtle to turn 45° to its right.

st The *show turtle* command shows the turtle on the computer screen.

ht The *bide turtle* command hides the turtle. You will not see the turtle again until you type the st command.

pu The *pen up* command tells the turtle to lift its drawing pen, so you can move the turtle without making marks on the screen.

pd The *pen down* command tells the turtle to put its pen down, so you can begin drawing.

6.1 Drawing with Logo

In Problem 6.1, you use Logo to create some designs. If you don't have a computer to work on, you can do the problem using a pencil and paper. It might be easiest to work on grid paper. You could let each square represent 10 turtle steps.

Problem 6.1

Spend some time exploring the kinds of shapes and designs you can make with combinations of Logo commands. For example, you might try to draw letters or designs like those below. Try writing commands to draw the initials of your name.

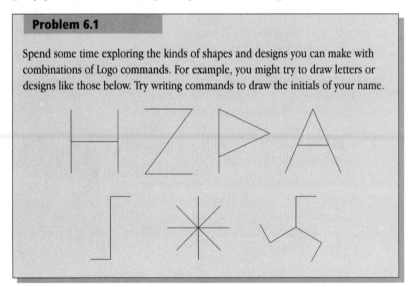

Problem 6.1 Follow-Up

The challenge of writing Logo commands to draw a desired design can be used to make a game for two players or two teams. One player could draw a design and challenge the other player to write Logo commands that will make that design. Or, one player could write some Logo commands and challenge the other player to sketch the design the commands will produce. Work with students in your group to make rules for a Turtle Challenge Game. Play the game you create, and modify the rules to improve the game.

6.2 Debugging Computer Programs

A set of computer commands that performs a task is called a *computer program*. In Problem 6.1, you wrote short computer programs to make some designs.

Computer programs usually won't run perfectly the first time you try them. Programs that don't run the way you expect them to are said to have "bugs" in them. You can "debug" your programs so that they run properly.

To debug a Logo program, use your computer mouse or the arrow keys to move to a command you want to change. Use the **delete** key to remove any words or numbers you want to change. Type in the new words or numbers, and then press the **return** key to see the turtle follow your new instructions.

> ### Problem 6.2
>
> In this problem, you will write a Logo computer program to draw a triangle. Follow these steps:
>
> - On a piece of paper, write a Logo program that you think will draw a triangle.
> - Type your Logo program into the computer.
> - Debug your program. Keep making changes in your program until you have produced a triangle.
> - Write down your new, debugged program for drawing a triangle.

Problem 6.2 Follow-Up

Were you surprised by anything as you wrote and debugged your triangle program?

Answers to Problem 6.2

Programs will vary.

Answer to Problem 6.2 Follow-Up

Answers will vary.

6.2

Debugging Computer Programs

At a Glance

Grouping:
Small Groups

Launch

- Make sure students understand how to edit commands.

Explore

- Allow groups to write, enter, and debug programs to draw a triangle. (If you have only a demonstration computer, do this as a class activity.)

Summarize

- In a class discussion, have students share what they discovered while writing and debugging their programs.

- Have some groups demonstrate their programs. (*optional*)

Assignment Choices

ACE questions 5–11 and unassigned choices from earlier problems

6.3

Making Polygons

Grouping:
Small Groups

Launch

- Explain that students will use their knowledge of the properties of quadrilaterals to write Logo programs.

Explore

- Allow groups to write and debug programs to draw the various quadrilaterals.

Summarize

- Choose groups to demonstrate their programs or (if you have only a demonstration computer) edit groups' programs as a class.

6.3 **Making Polygons**

In earlier parts of this unit, you have seen that interesting designs often begin with simple shapes like triangles, squares, and rectangles. In this problem, you write Logo commands to make these basic shapes. If you don't have a computer, you can do this problem using a pencil and paper.

> **Problem 6.3**
>
> Write Logo programs to make each of the following shapes. Experiment at the computer to test and debug your programs. Each shape can be made in lots of different ways.
>
> **A.** A square with sides of length 50
>
> **B.** A rectangle with sides of length 50 and 100
>
> **C.** A parallelogram—but not a rectangle—with sides of length 80 and 30
>
> **D.** A parallelogram—but not a square—with all sides of length 70

■ **Problem 6.3 Follow-Up**

1. Explain how you used what you know about the measures of sides and angles of squares to help you write your programs.
2. Explain how you used what you know about the measures of sides and angles of rectangles to help you write your programs.
3. Explain how you used what you know about the measures of sides and angles of parallelograms to help you write your programs.

Assignment Choices

ACE questions 18–25 and unassigned choices from earlier problems

Assessment

It is appropriate to use the Quiz after this problem.

Answers to Problem 6.3

See page 75g.

Answers to Problem 6.3 Follow-Up

See page 75h.

As you work on these ACE questions, use your calculator whenever you need it.

Applications

In 1–4, sketch the shape that each Logo program will produce. Use arrows to show the direction the turtle moves around the figure. If possible, check your answers on the computer.

1.
```
fd 50
rt 90
fd 100
rt 90
fd 50
rt 90
fd 100
```

2.
```
fd 100
lt 45
fd 70
lt 90
fd 70
lt 45
fd 100
lt 90
fd 100
```

3.
```
fd 100
lt 120
fd 40
lt 120
fd 40
```

4.
```
fd 100
rt 30
bk 50
lt 30
fd 25
rt 30
bk 10
```

In 5–8, write a Logo program that will produce the given shape.

5.

6.

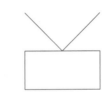

7.

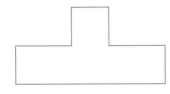

8.

1.

2.

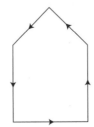

3.

4.

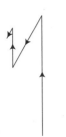

Answers

Applications

1. See below left.
2. See below left.
3. See below left.
4. See below left.
5. Possible program:

   ```
   fd 100
   bk 200
   fd 100
   rt 90
   fd 100
   bk 200
   ```

6. Possible program:

   ```
   lt 45
   fd 75
   bk 75
   rt 90
   fd 75
   bk 75
   rt 45
   fd 50
   rt 90
   fd 50
   rt 90
   fd 100
   rt 90
   fd 50
   rt 90
   fd 50
   ```

7. Possible program:

```
fd 50
rt 90
fd 75
lt 90
fd 50
rt 90
fd 50
rt 90
fd 50
lt 90
fd 75
rt 90
fd 50
rt 90
fd 200
```

8. Possible program:

```
rt 30
fd 100
rt 60
fd 100
rt 60
fd 100
rt 120
fd 200
```

Connections

9a. See below right.

9b. See below right.

Connections

In 9–11, a Logo program and the shape it created are given. Parts a and b show the same program, but with a bug (the bug is the command in bold print). Explain how the bug would affect the shape the program would draw.

9.

▢ ▦ Command ▦	▤▢ ▦▦▦ square ▦▦▦
`fd 100` ⇧	
`rt 90`	
`fd 100`	
`rt 90`	
`fd 100`	
`rt 90`	
`fd 100`	
`rt 90`	

a.
```
fd 100
rt 80
fd 100
rt 90
fd 100
rt 90
fd 100
rt 90
```

b.
```
fd 120
rt 90
fd 100
rt 90
fd 100
rt 90
fd 100
rt 90
```

9a. Possible answer: The bug makes one angle too large so the square does not close.

9b. Possible answer: The bug makes one side of the square too long.

10.

```
┌─▣░Command░───┬─┬──┬─▤□──────rectangle──────┐
│ fd 100      ⇧│ │  │                         │
│ rt 90        │ │  │                         │
│ fd 70        │ │  │                         │
│ rt 90        │ │  │                         │
│ fd 100       │ │  │          ┌──────┐       │
│ rt 90        │ │  │          │      │       │
│ fd 70        │ │  │          │      │       │
│ rt 90        │ │  │          │      │       │
│              │ │  │          │      │       │
│              │ │  │         🐢└──────┘       │
│              │ │  │                         │
│             ⇩│ │  │                         │
│             ▣│ │  │                         │
└──────────────┴─┴──┴─────────────────────────┘
```

a. fd 100
      rt 90
      fd 70
      rt 90
      fd 100
      rt 90
      fd 60
      rt 90

b. fd 100
      rt 20
      fd 70
      rt 90
      fd 100
      rt 90
      fd 70
      rt 90

10a. See below left.

10b. See below left.

10a. Possible answer: The bug makes one side of the rectangle too short.

10b. Possible answer: The bug makes one angle too large so the rectangle does not close.

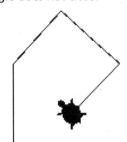

11a. See below right.

11b. See below right.

11.

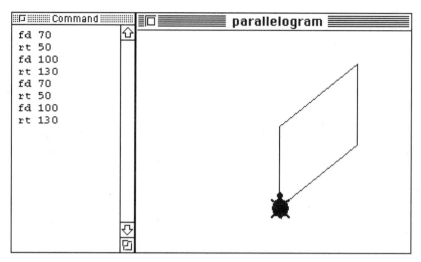

```
 ▦ Command ▦
fd 70
rt 50
fd 100
rt 130
fd 70
rt 50
fd 100
rt 130
```

parallelogram

a.
```
fd 70
rt 50
fd 100
rt 110
fd 70
rt 50
fd 100
rt 130
```

b.
```
fd 70
rt 50
fd 100
rt 130
fd 40
rt 50
fd 100
rt 130
```

11a. Possible answer: The bug makes one angle too large so the parallelogram does not close.

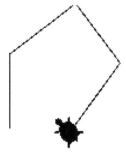

11b. Possible answer: The bug makes one side of the parallelogram too short.

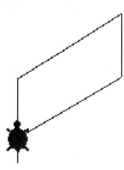

12. Suppose the turtle understood only the command for a 30° turn. What turns could you make by combining 30° turns?

13. Suppose the turtle understood only the command for a 45° turn. What turns could you make by combining 45° turns?

14. Suppose the turtle understood only the commands for 30° and 45° turns. What turns could you make by combining 30° and 45° turns?

15. Suppose the turtle understood only the command for a move of 10 steps. What moves could you make by combining 10-step moves?

16. Suppose the turtle understood only the command for a move of 15 steps. What moves could you make by combining 15-step moves?

17. Suppose the turtle understood only the commands for moves of 10 and 15 steps. What moves could you make by combining 10-step and 15-step moves?

Extensions

Questions 18–25 involve the `repeat` command. You use `repeat` to tell the turtle to follow a set of instructions a specified number of times. For example, the command `repeat 3 [rt 60 fd 40]` tells the turtle to follow the instructions `rt 60 fd 40` three times. Be sure to put spaces between the words and numbers and to put square brackets around the instructions to be repeated.

In 18–21, sketch the figure that the Logo commands would create.

18. `repeat 4 [fd 60 lt 90]`

19. `repeat 4 [fd 50 rt 90 fd 50 lt 90]`

20. `repeat 3 [fd 100 lt 120]`

21. `repeat 8 [fd 80 bk 80 rt 45]`

---

12. The turtle could make turns with measures that are multiples of 30—that is, 30°, 60°, 90°, 120°, 150°, . . .

13. The turtle could make turns with measures that are multiples of 45—that is, 45°, 90°, 135°, 180°, 225°, . . .

14. By combining left and right turns, the turtle could make turns that are multiples of 15°—that is, 15°, 30°, 45°, 60°, 75°, . . .

15. The turtle could move forward or backward by multiples of 10 steps—that is, 10 steps, 20 steps, 30 steps, 40 steps, 50 steps, . . .

16. The turtle could move forward or backward by multiples of 15 steps—that is, 15 steps, 30 steps, 45 steps, 60 steps, 75 steps, . . .

17. By combining forward and backward moves, the turtle could move by multiples of 5 steps—that is, 5 steps, 10 steps, 15 steps, 20 steps, 25 steps, . . .

Extensions

18.

19. See below left.

20. See below left.

21. See page 75h.

19.

20.

22a. Possible program:
```
repeat 4 [fd 100 rt 90]
```

22b. Since all the sides are equal and all the angles are the same, you can write commands for one side and one angle and repeat them four times.

23a. Possible program:
```
repeat 2 [fd 100 rt 90 fd 70 rt 90]
```

23b. Since opposite sides are the same length and opposite angles have the same measure, you can write the commands to draw a long side, an angle, a short side, and an angle, and then repeat them twice.

24a. Possible program:
```
repeat 2 [fd 70 rt 50 fd 100 rt 130]
```

24b. Since opposite sides are the same length and opposite angles have the same measure, you can write the commands to draw a short side, an angle, a long side, and an angle, and then repeat them twice.

25. Possible program:
```
repeat 60 [fd 50 bk 50 rt 6]
```

In 22–24, you are given Logo programs for drawing a square, a rectangle, and a parallelogram. Each of those programs can be shortened by using the repeat command.

22. **a.** Write a shortened program for drawing the square in question 9.

   b. Explain how properties of squares make it possible to write a shorter program using repeat.

23. **a.** Write a shortened program for drawing the rectangle in question 10.

   b. Explain how properties of rectangles make it possible to write a shorter program using repeat.

24. **a.** Write a shortened program for drawing the parallelogram in question 11.

   b. Explain how properties of parallelograms make it possible to write a shorter program using repeat.

25. Write a Logo program that uses the repeat command to make a starburst design similar to the one below.

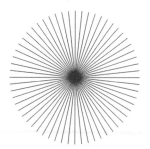

Mathematical Reflections

Use what you have learned in *Shapes and Designs* to write a geometric description of each object pictured below. Be sure to discuss

* the shapes, angles, and symmetry in the object
* possible reasons why the object has the shape that it does

A.

B.

C.

D.

Have you seen any new shapes and designs to add to your collection? Remember to write about all your discoveries in your journal!

Tip for the Linguistically Diverse Classroom

Dissection The Dissection technique is described in detail in *Getting to Know Connected Mathematics*. It involves highlighting, circling, or "lifting" part of picture to respond to a question. Example: Item A—A student might draw a bicycle like the one in the picture, then "lift" the frame part of the bicycle to the right showing it as a triangle and "lift" a wheel to the side showing it as a circle labeled 360°.

Possible Answers

a. Students may see a triangle, a trapezoid, and a pentagon. They may discuss the symmetry of the bike seat. They may point out the parallel lines on the trapezoid. Bicycle frames tend to employ triangles because they can maintain their shape even under a great deal of stress.

b. There are squares and rectangles in the window, and all of its angles are 90°. There is a line of symmetry in both the vertical and horizontal directions. Rectangular windows are very common because they are easy to construct and easy to open and close.

c. There are four turn symmetries for the face of the fan: 90°, 180°, 270°, and 360°. The fan blades make a circular path, and the circular housing is the shape that takes up the least space.

d. The web has many angles that meet at its center. The lines connecting the sides of the angles seem to form a series of overlapping triangles. These triangles would give the web stability. Some students may also see lines of symmetry in the web.

TEACHING THE INVESTIGATION

6.1 • Drawing with Logo

Students may think of computers as being useful for fast calculations or for keeping track of information. That computers can "do geometry" may be a big—and pleasant—surprise.

Launch

One of the best ways to introduce Logo is to have students act out Logo commands in the classroom. You might choose a student to be the "turtle" and have other students give the turtle directions to move about the classroom. Students could guide the turtle to the board, out the door, or to some other location.

After the "human turtle" demonstration, show students the computer turtle. Start the *Turtle Math* program and choose the Free Explore option. All the Logo activities in this investigation use the this option. The Free Explore screen is shown below.

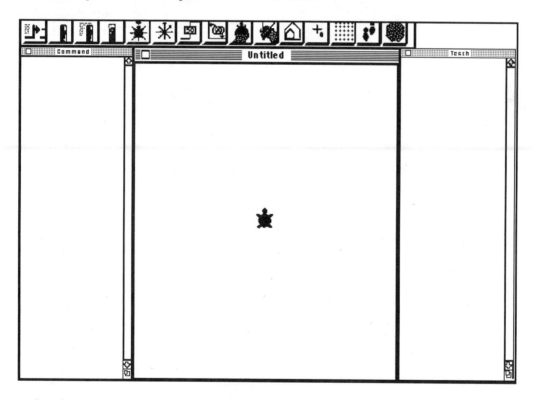

Explain that Logo commands are entered in the Command window and that the turtle moves in the Drawing window (labeled Untitled above). The Teach window will not be used in this investigation. The row of pictures along the top of the screen is the tool bar. The only tool students may need is the Erase All tool (the third tool from the left). The Erase All tool erases all the commands in the window and returns the turtle to its starting position.

Introduce the commands for moving the turtle (fd, bk, rt, and lt). Point out that each time you press the **return** key, the turtle acts out the command you have just typed in.

You might demonstrate how to use Logo commands to draw a square. Here is one program that will draw a square:

You might demonstrate how to use Logo commands to draw a square. Here is one program that will draw a square:

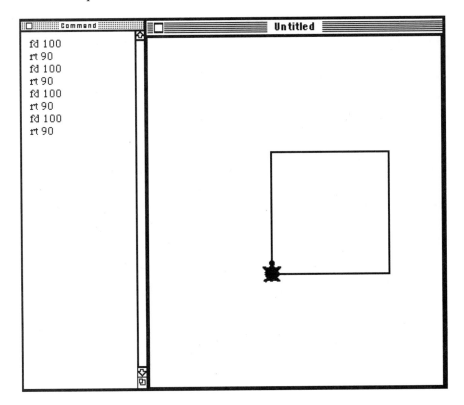

```
Command
fd 100
rt 90
fd 100
rt 90
fd 100
rt 90
fd 100
rt 90
```

Tell students that you want to instruct the turtle to draw a square with sides of length 100.

We can start by telling the turtle to walk forward 100 steps.

Type fd 100 in the Command window, and press the **return** key. The turtle will move forward 100 "steps."

Now we need to tell the turtle to turn. How many degrees does the turtle need to turn? What command should I give the turtle?

Students should see that, since a square has 90° angles, the turn should be 90°. The turtle can turn to the right or to the left, so the command should be rt 90 or lt 90. Type in either command, and press the **return** key.

For the Teacher: Steps vs. Turns

Initially your students may be confused by the two types of turtle moves: *steps* and *turns*. Often students will misinterpret the turns, rt and lt, as steps. They might think, for example, that rt 90 means "go right 90 steps." You may need to remind them that the turtle can only do one thing at a time, either change direction or move. If students suggest an incorrect command during your demonstration, you may choose to type it anyway as an opportunity to show students how to correct commands.

The turtle is now facing in the correct direction, so we can tell it to move forward to draw the second side of the square. What command should I type in now?

Help students to see that, since all sides of a square are equal, the turtle needs to move forward 100 steps. Type `fd 100`, and press the **return** key. Continue asking students what you should do next and typing in commands until the square is complete.

Now I can type `ht` to hide the turtle, so that we can see the entire square.

Type `ht` and press the **return** key.

Now, what if I want to change my drawing? For example, suppose I want the first segment that the turtle draws to be 50 units long instead of 100. Which command do I need to change?

Help students to see that you would need to change the first command from `fd 100` to `fd 50`. Use the mouse to move to the first line in the Command window. Erase the `100`, type in `50`, and press the **return** key. The picture in the Drawing window will now look something like this:

Notice that when I changed the command and pressed **return,** the turtle redid all the steps to draw a new figure.

You may want to show some more examples to help your students become proficient entering and editing commands. When you feel students are ready, allow them to work on Problem 6.1.

Explore

If enough computers are available, allow students to work in small groups at the computers. If you have only a few computers, some groups could work at them, while others work with pencil and paper; they could switch halfway through the allotted class time. If no computers are available for students to use, have them write their programs and draw their designs with pencil and paper.

If you want students to spend more time making computer designs, have them work on the game in Problem 6.1 Follow-Up.

Summarize

Set up the demonstration computer, and allow each group to show a design they have made. If your students have done all their work with pencil and paper, some of their designs may not turn out how they expect. If this occurs, work as a class to edit the commands to produce the intended design.

6.2 • Debugging Computer Programs

Problem 6.2 allows students to observe how changing individual commands alters their drawings. It also begins to lay the groundwork for understanding exterior angles since the turtle turns through the exterior, not the interior, angle.

We also hope that students learn to see "bugs" as intriguing things to think about, not as mistakes!

Launch

If you have only a demonstration computer, you can do this problem as a class activity.

turn of turtle

In Problem 6.1, you wrote Logo commands to create some designs. Each set of commands you wrote to create a design is an example of a *computer program*.

You may have found that your computer programs did not work exactly the way you wanted them to the first time you typed them into the computer. When a program does not work the way we want it to, we say it has a *bug*.

If a program you write has a bug in it, how can you fix it?

Students should say that you use the mouse to move to the incorrect command and correct it. When you press the **return** key, the turtle will follow the new, corrected commands. If you feel your students need more help to understand how to edit a program, you may want to show them some examples.

Explore

Students should write their program on paper *before* they type it into the computer. Writing a Logo program to draw a triangle is a challenge. Our intention is that students will probably write a procedure on paper that does *not* produce a triangle. Once they have entered the program into the computer, they will need to edit it until it draws a triangle.

If you have only a computer for demonstration, you can do Problem 6.2 as a class activity. Write a program at the board, asking students to suggest commands. Then type the program in, and work as a class to debug it.

Encourage your students to type in the program exactly as they have written it. Any set of instructions that produces a figure with three sides and two or more angle turns can easily be edited to produce a triangle.

Here is an example of what you might expect. Luisa and Mei-lin worked together to write this program:

```
fd 100
rt 60
fd 100
rt 60
fd 100
```

After they typed in their program, the computer displayed this picture. Notice that the turtle is mostly off the screen, and the drawing does not look at all like a triangle.

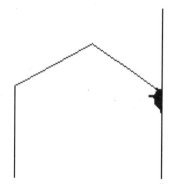

Luisa and Mei-lin began to debug their program. They used the mouse to move to the second rt 60 command. After some lively debate, they changed rt 60 to rt 100 and pressed the **return** key.

Next, they decided to increase the angle even more, and changed the rt 100 to rt 150. After pressing the **return** key, they saw this drawing:

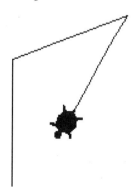

They decided that the angle looked about right, but they wanted to make the third side longer. They changed the last `fd  100` command in, first to `fd  150`, then to `fd  160`:

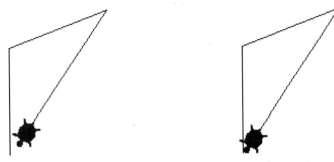

At this point, they thought they were done. However, when they showed their triangle to the students at the next computer, they were challenged to hide their turtle using the `ht` command, which produced this drawing:

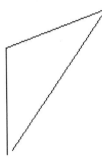

Luisa and Mei-lin then went back to the `fd  160` command and changed it to `fd  170`, producing this (almost complete) triangle:

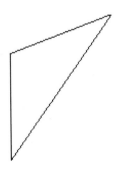

They decided this was as close as they would get, so they wrote down their new, debugged program:

```
fd 100
rt 60
fd 100
rt 150
fd 170
```

Notice that Luisa and Mei-lin used trial and error, instead of precise calculations, to produce their picture. That is perfectly appropriate at this point.

Summarize

Hold a class discussion in which students share what they discovered while writing and debugging their programs. You might have some groups demonstrate their programs at the computer.

6.3 • Making Polygons

In this problem, students write, test, and debug Logo programs that draw various quadrilaterals.

Launch

Explain to your students that, in this problem, they will use what they have learned about the measures of sides and angles of quadrilaterals to write some Logo programs.

Explore

Let students work in small groups on Problem 6.3. If enough computers are available, allows students to work in small groups at the computers. If you have only a few computers, some groups could work at the computers while others work with pencil and paper; they could switch halfway through the allotted class time. If no computers are available for students to use, have students write their programs and draw their designs with pencil and paper.

Summarize

Choose groups of students to present their programs at the demonstration computer. When a presentation is done, ask if any groups wrote a different program to make the quadrilateral. If students have done all their work with a pencil and paper, some of the designs may not turn out the way they expect. Work as a class to edit the commands to produce the intended quadrilateral.

Additional Answers

Answers to Problem 6.3

A. Possible program:
```
fd 50
rt 90
fd 50
rt 90
fd 50
rt 90
fd 50
```

B. Possible program:
```
fd 50
rt 90
fd 100
rt 90
fd 50
rt 90
fd 100
```

C. Possible program:
```
rt 60
fd 80
rt 120
fd 30
rt 60
fd 80
rt 120
fd 30
```

D. Possible program:
```
rt 91
fd 70
rt 89
fd 70
rt 91
fd 70
rt 89
fd 70
```

Answers to Problem 6.3 Follow-Up

1. In a square, all sides are equal and all angles are 90°. In the square in part A, all sides are 50 steps long, so the commands must alternate between 50-step moves and 90° turns.

2. In a rectangle, opposite sides are equal and all angles are 90°. In the rectangle in part B, one pair of opposite sides are each 50 steps long, and the other pair are each 100 steps long. The commands must alternate between steps and 90° turns, and the step commands must alternate between 50 steps and 100 steps.

3. In a parallelogram, opposite sides and opposite angles are equal, and the angle sum is 360°. In the parallelogram in part C, one pair of opposite sides are each 80 steps long and the other pair are each 30 steps long. Every other turn must be the same, since opposite angles are equal. Commands must alternate between steps and turns, and the angle measures and step lengths must alternate. In the parallelogram in part D, commands must alternate between turns and 70-step moves. Every other turn must be the same, since opposite angles are equal.

ACE Answers

Extensions

21.

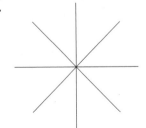

Assigning the Unit Project

The unit project, What I Know About Shapes and Designs, is an integral part of the assessment in *Shapes and Designs*. The project—which asks students to synthesize and summarize their learning from the unit—is introduced prior to Investigation 1.

As you near the end of the unit, discuss the project with the students in detail. Their collection of information should be close to complete, and they should begin thinking about how to present the information.

Encourage students to consider a wide variety of formats for presenting their ideas—such as a story, a report, a book, a movie, a slide show, a poster or set of posters, or a mobile. You might suggest that students locate books about architecture and design in the library to help stimulate ideas. Stress that you expect them to use the vocabulary and concepts from the unit to show everything they know about the set of shapes they have been considering and about what they have learned. Although students should be encouraged to be creative, the emphasis of the project should be on mathematical content.

Samples of student projects and a suggested scoring rubric are given in the Assessment Resources section.

The Unit Project

What I Know About Shapes and Designs

At the beginning of this unit, you were asked to think about the characteristics of different shapes and how unusual a shape can be and still be a triangle, quadrilateral, pentagon, or hexagon. You were also asked to think about the relationships among these shapes. It is now time to design your final project.

You can present your project in several different forms or combinations of forms. You may decide to present your information as a book, a poster or a set of posters, a story, a report, a mobile, a movie, a slide show, or any other appropriate form that you design. Whatever form you choose, remember that what you have to demonstrate and explain in your project are the following things:

- The characteristics of the following shapes: triangles, squares, rectangles, parallelograms, quadrilaterals, pentagons, hexagons, octagons
- The relationships among the shapes listed above
- Examples of places where these shapes can be found in your world.

Use the information you have collected, plus what you learned from your study of this unit, to prepare your final project. Be certain your project shows

- All the facts you know about the relations among the sides of polygons. Consider properties of all polygons and properties of special polygons, such as squares, rectangles, and other parallelograms.
- All the facts you know about the relations among angles of polygons. Again, consider properties of all polygons and properties of special polygons.

Assessment Resources

Check-Up 1

In 1–5, decide whether the given statement is true or false. Give explanations or sketches to support your answers.

1. With side lengths 6, 8, and 10, there is one and only one triangle shape that can be made.

2. Any two quadrilaterals that have sides of the same lengths will be identical in size and shape. For example, two quadrilaterals with side lengths 5, 7, 9, and 11 will be the same size and shape.

3. There can be no pentagon with sides lengths 2, 2, 3, 7, and 15.

4. All rectangles are special kinds of parallelograms.

5. All parallelograms are special kinds of squares.

In 6–8, use an angle ruler to measure each angle.

6.

7.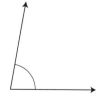

8.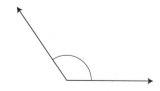

Check-Up 1

In 9 and 10, draw an angle with the given measure.

9. 90°   **10.** 150°

One of the most common places we see angles is on the faces of clocks. At the start of each hour, the minute hand is pointed straight up, at the 12. In 11–13, mark where the minute hand is at the start of an hour as one side of an angle. Sketch the angle formed by the minute hand at the time shown, and give the measure of the angle.

11. 10 minutes   **12.** 45 minutes   **13.** 25 minutes

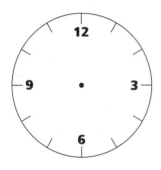   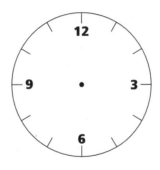   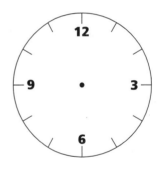

  angle = _____   angle = _____   angle = _____

Check-Up 2

In 1–4, decide whether the given statements are true or false. Give explanations or sketches to support your answers.

1. You can always completely surround a point by placing the vertices of four squares together.

2. The sum of the measures of the angles of any triangle is 90°.

3. In a regular hexagon, all sides are the same length and all angles are 100°.

4. Any triangle can be used to tile a flat surface.

5. Use shapes A, B, C, D, E, or F from your Shapes Set to answer a–c.

    a. Choose a single shape and show how it tiles.

    b. Choose a single shape and show how it does not tile.

Check-Up 2

c. Explain why the one shape you chose did tile and the other shape you chose did not tile.

In 6–9, use the given data and what you know about relations among sides and angles to find the lengths and angle measurements of all sides and angles in the figures.

6. square

2 cm

7. rectangle

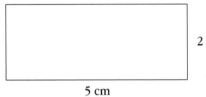

2 cm

5 cm

8. parallelogram

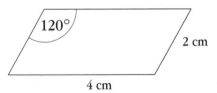

120°

2 cm

4 cm

9. parallelogram

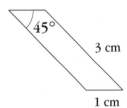

45°

3 cm

1 cm

Names _____ Date _____

Below is the face of a compass. It is standard practice to match each compass direction with the degree measure of the angle formed by a clockwise turn from due north (N) to the desired direction. For example, east (E) is given the direction number 90°.

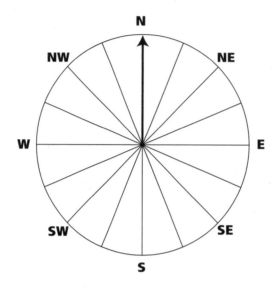

In 1–8, find the direction number for the given point of the compass.

1. NE (northeast)

2. SE (southeast)

3. S (south)

4. SW (southwest)

5. W (west)

6. NW (northwest)

7. N (north)

8. NNE (north-northeast, between N and NE)

In 9 and 10, show all the line symmetries and give the degree measures for all the turn symmetries for the given shape from your Shapes Set.

9. shape C

Quiz

10. shape K

11. Jack has made a tiling with quadrilateral shapes. Jack can pick up a shape from his tiling and turn it 90°, and it will fit back where it was. Kenesha has used a different quadrilateral to make a tiling. Kenesha's quadrilateral will not fit back into the pattern when she turns it 90°.

   a. What might Jack's quadrilateral look like? Draw or describe it, and explain why it works.

   b. What might Kenesha's quadrilateral look like? Draw or describe it, and explain why it doesn't fit back into the tiling pattern when it is turned 90°.

Quiz

In 12 and 13, given the computer code, what figure will be drawn?

12. fd 25
    rt 120
    fd 25
    rt 120
    fd 25

13. rt 60
    fd 100
    rt 90
    fd 100
    rt 90
    fd 100
    rt 90
    fd 100

In 14–17, use the shapes on the following page.

14. The figures I, L, and V can be grouped together, but X would not belong in the group. Explain why.

15. The figures E, G, H, I, and M can be grouped together, but S would not belong in the group. Explain why.

16. The figures F, Q, W, and X can be grouped together, but N would not belong in the group. Explain why.

17. The figures A, B, H, J, M, S, and U can be grouped together, but N would not belong in the group. Explain why.

Quiz

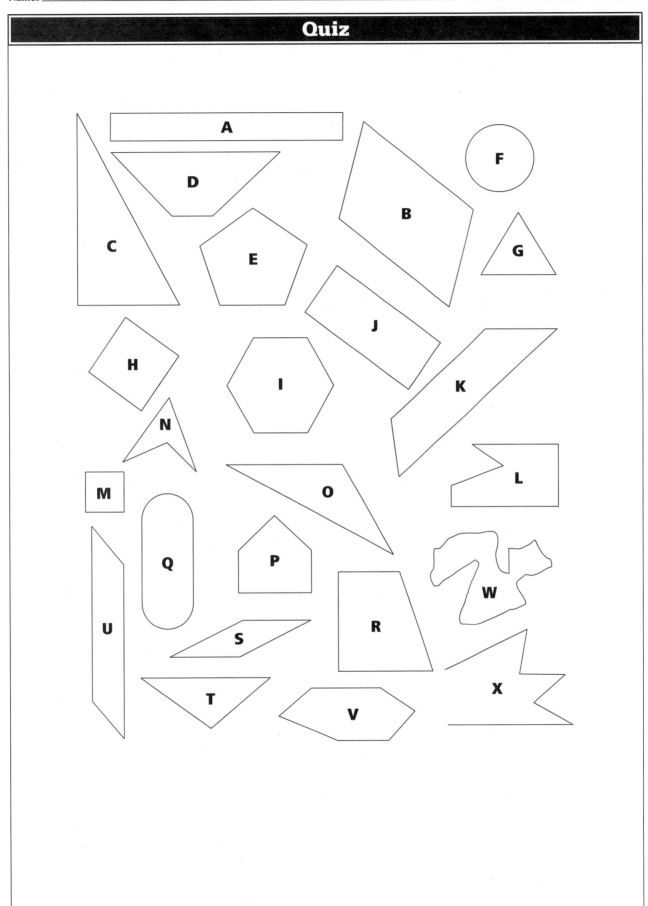

Assign these questions as additional homework, or use them as review, quiz, or test questions.

1. Spread your fingers and look at the angles created by them. In a–c, use your angle ruler to measure the angles formed by the given fingers. (To take the measure, lay your hand flat on your desk and spread the fingers you are measuring as far as possible.)

   a. Your thumb and first finger

   b. Your index and middle finger

   c. Your thumb and pinkie finger

   d. How do your measurements for a, b, and c compare?

2. Naomi picked 3, 6, 6, and 12 for the side lengths of a quadrilateral. Marcelo says she cannot make a quadrilateral with these lengths. Is he right? Explain.

In 3–5, decide whether the given statement is true or false. Give explanations or sketches to support your answers.

3. A quadrilateral with sides 5, 8, 5, 8, in that order, is always a rectangle.

4. A quadrilateral with two sides of 7 and two sides of 11 is always a parallelogram.

5. You will always be able to draw two different triangles using side lengths of 3, 4, and 5.

In 6–8, use a coordinate grid like the one shown below.

6. If a line segment connecting (4, 3) and (7, 6) forms one *side* of a square, what might be the coordinates of the other corners of that square?

7. If (2, 0) and (5, 5) are two vertices of a triangle that does not have a right angle, what might be the coordinates of the other vertex of that triangle?

8. Draw your triangle for question 7. For each angle of the triangle, tell whether the angles are greater than or less than 90°.

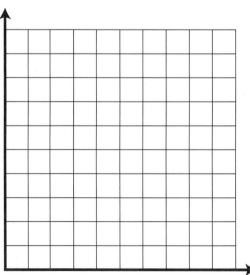

9. Alejandro's dad bought pentagon tiles to tile his patio. When he returned with the tiles and showed them to Alejandro, Alejandro told him that he would have to go back for another shape tile to go with the pentagon tiles or exchange the pentagon tiles for a different shape altogether, because the pentagon alone would not work to tile the patio. Was Alejandro correct? Why or why not?

10. G. Oni Ometer is a math rap singer who lives in Miami, Florida. She is starting a fall concert tour, and she flies her own plane to every concert. Here is her tour schedule:

Dallas, Texas	September 14–16
Boston, Massachusetts	September 18–20
San Diego, California	September 22–25
Detroit, Michigan	September 27–30
Miami, Florida	October 2–8

To fly from one city to the next, G. Oni needs a flight angle and compass direction to direct her plane. A flight angle is formed by a two lines that start in the city from which the flight takes off. One line points north, and the other points to the flight's destination. The flight angles are labeled with degree measure and west or east. For example, to fly from Miami to Dallas for the first concert, G. Oni flies along a 71° west flight angle. Using your angle ruler and the map below, find the fight angles for the rest of G. Oni's concert tour.

Name _____ Date _____

1. **a.** Is the triangle at the right a regular polygon? Explain why or why not.

    b. Could this triangle be used to tile a surface? Explain why or why not.

2. An equilateral triangle has a perimeter of 12. What is the length of each side? Explain your reasoning.

3. A square has a perimeter of 16.4 centimeters. What is the length of each side? Explain your reasoning

4. For each of the shapes below, find the unknown angle measure without using your angle ruler.

    a. 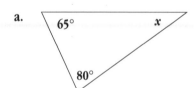   **b.** 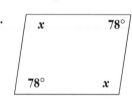   **c.**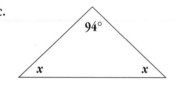

5. Is it possible for a parallelogram to have a 54° angle and a 126° angle? Explain why or why not.

    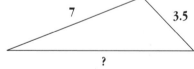

6. Use the triangle at right to answer the following questions.

    a. Ted estimates that the unknown side length is 11. How do you think his estimate compares with the actual length? Explain your reasoning.

    b. Felicia estimates that the unknown side length is 6.75. How do you think her estimate compares with the actual length? Explain your reasoning.

    c. Make your own estimate of the unknown side length. Explain your strategy for finding your estimate, and explain why you think your estimate is reasonable.

7. A rectangle has a perimeter of 42 centimeters. One of its sides is 11 centimeters long. What are the dimensions of the rectangle? Explain your answer.

8. Is it possible for a triangle to have angles with measures 34°, 45°, and 100°?

9. In the diagram below, what are the measures of the five angles?

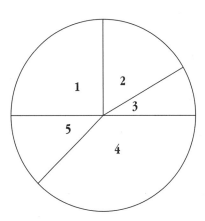

10. Refer to the Logo program to answer the following questions.

```
rt 30
fd 90
rt 60
fd 120
rt 120
fd 90
rt 60
fd 120
```

a. If you run this program, what kind of figure will it draw?

b. What is the sum of the side lengths of the figure in turtle steps?

c. What are the measures of the angles of the figure?

Name _____ Date _____

Notebook Checklist

Journal Organization

_____ Problems and Mathematical Reflections are labeled and dated.

_____ Work is neat and easy to find and follow.

Vocabulary

_____ All words are listed.

_____ All words are defined or described.

Quizzes and Check-Ups

_____ Quiz   _____ Check-Up 1   _____ Check-Up 2

Homework Assignments

_____ _____

_____ _____

_____ _____

_____ _____

_____ _____

_____ _____

_____ _____

_____ _____

_____ _____

_____ _____

_____ _____

_____ _____

_____ _____

_____ _____

_____ _____

Self-Assessment

Vocabulary

Of the vocabulary words I defined or described in my journal, the word _____ best demonstrates my ability to give a clear definition or description.

Of the vocabulary words I defined or described in my journal, the word _____ best demonstrates my ability to use an example to help explain or describe an idea.

Mathematical Ideas

1. **a.** I learned these things about how sides and angles form shapes of polygons:

    b. Here are page numbers of journal entries that give evidence of what I have learned, along with descriptions of what each entry shows:

2. **a.** These are the mathematical ideas I am still struggling with:

    b. This is why I think these ideas are difficult for me:

    c. Here are page numbers of journal entries that give evidence of what I am struggling with, along with descriptions of what each entry shows:

Class Participation

I contributed to the classroom discussion and understanding of *Shapes and Designs* when I…
(Give examples.)

Answer Keys

Answers to Check-Up 1

1. true; Three sides can form only one triangle. This triangle can be flipped or turned so that it looks slightly different because of its orientation, but it is still the same triangle.

2. false; It is possible to sequence the four line segments in more than one arrangement, such as 5–7–9–11 or 5–9–7–11 or 5–9–11–7. Also, any quadrilateral can be "squished" into different-shaped quadrilaterals.

3. true; The sum of the four short sides (2 + 2 + 3 + 7) is less than the longest side (15), so it would not be possible for the sides to connect.

4. true; To be a parallelogram, a figure must have four sides, with opposite sides equal and opposite angles equal. A rectangle meets these requirements and has the additional requirement that all four of its angles are 90°.

5. false; Not every parallelogram has four equal sides, or four 90° angles; however, a square is a special parallelogram.

6. about 20°

7. about 80°

8. about 125°

9.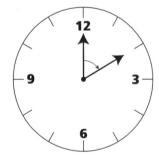

10.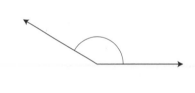

11. 60°   12. 270°   13. 150°

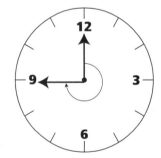
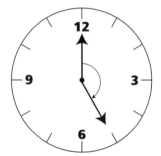

Answers to Check-Up 2

1. true; The angles that fit around a single point must add to 360°. Because a square has 90° angles and the sum of four 90° angles is 360°, this will work.

2. false; The sum of the measures of the angles of any triangle is 180°.

3. false; In a regular hexagon, all angles are 120°.

4. true; Because the sum of the angles in any triangle is 180°, the sum of the angles of two triangles is 360°, so six copies of a the triangle will fit around a point with two copies of each angle around the point.

5. **a.** Answers will vary. Students could have used shape A (the triangle), B (the square), or D (the hexagon).

   b. Answers will vary. Students could have used shape C (the pentagon), E (the heptagon), or F (the octagon).

   c. Because the measures of the angles of the triangle, square, and hexagon are factors of 360, multiples of them will fit around a vertex point. The angles of the pentagon, septagon, and octagon are not factors of 360.

6. All sides are 2 cm and all angles are 90°.

7. Opposite sides must be of equal length, so the short side is 2 cm and the long side is 5 cm, and all angles are 90°.

8. Opposite sides must be of equal length, so the short side is 2 cm and the long side is 4 cm. Opposite angles must be equal, so the other obtuse angle is 120°. The two acute angles are equal, and each must be $\frac{360 - 240}{2} = 60°$.

9. Opposite sides must be of equal length, so the short side is 1 cm and the long side is 3 cm. Opposite angles must be equal, so the other acute angle is 45°. The two obtuse angles are equal, and each must be $\frac{360 - 90}{2} = 135°$.

Answers to Quiz

1. 45°
2. 135°
3. 180°
4. 225°
5. 270°
6. 315°
7. 0°
8. 22.5°

9. C, the pentagon, has five lines of symmetry, the lines connecting each vertex to the midpoint of the opposite side.

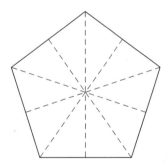

   The regular pentagon also has five turn symmetries: 72°, 144°, 216°, 288°, and 360°.

10. K, the rhombus, has two lines of symmetry, the two diagonals of the shape. There are also two turn symmetries: 180° and 360°.

11. **a.** Jack's shape must be a square. Because its sides and angles are the same measure, the square is the only quadrilateral that can be turned 90° and fit back in the same spot.

    b. Kenesha's shape could be any quadrilateral other than a square. For example, students may choose a rectangle or a parallelogram and show how the adjacent angles, being different sizes, make it impossible to fit back in the original space.

12. an equilateral triangle

13. a square

14. I, L, and V are all hexagons. X is not part of the group because, even though it has six line segments for sides, it is not a closed figure and therefore not a polygon.

15. E, G, H, I, and M are all regular polygons (all sides and all angles are equal). S is not part of the group because it is not a regular polygon; only its sides are equal.

16. F, Q, W, and X are all grouped together because they are not polygons. These figures are either not closed (X) or do not have straight-line sides (F, Q, and W). N is closed and has straight-line sides and is therefore a polygon.

17. At first glance it may appear that A, B, H, J, M, S, and U are grouped together because they are all quadrilaterals. Because N is also a quadrilateral means that one needs to look for something more specific. Thus A, B, H, J, M, S, and U are grouped together because they are also all parallelograms; N is not part of the group because it is not a parallelogram.

Answers to Question Bank

1.   **a.** Answers will vary. Students' measurements are typically between 75° and 90°.

    b. Answers will vary. Students' measurements are typically between 15° and 30°.

    c. Answers will vary. Students' measurements are typically between 105° and 120°.

    d. The angle for c is the largest. The angle for a is somewhat smaller. The angle for b is much smaller than the other two angles.

2. Marcelo is not right. You can make a quadrilateral with these four line segments since the sum of the three smallest sides (3 + 6 + 6) is greater than the length of the longest side (12).

3. false; It could be a rectangle or it could be just a parallelogram. Thus the "always" part of the statement is not true.

4. false; It could be a parallelogram if the sides were put together in 7–11–7–11 order. But if you put them together 7, 7, 11, 11, it would be a kite.

5. false; You can draw only one triangle of sides 3, 4, and 5. You can orient the figure in different ways, but it will always be a triangle with the same size and shape.

6. One possibility is (1, 6) and (4, 9); the other is (7, 0) and (10, 3).

7. Possible answer: (0, 5)

8. Answers will vary.

9. Alejandro was correct. The sum of the angles that fit together around a point must be 360°. All the angles of a regular pentagon are 108°, and multiples of 108 will not make 360.

10. Dallas to Boston, about 60° E; Boston to San Diego, about 105° W; San Diego to Detroit, about 75° E; Detroit to Miami, about 165° E

Answers to Unit Test

1. **a.** No, because all sides and angles of the triangle are not equal.

   b. Yes; Any triangle can be used to tile the plane.

2. Each side would have length $\frac{12}{3} = 4$.

3. Each side would have length $\frac{16.4}{4} = 4.1$.

4. **a.** $x = 35°$ **b.** $x = 102°$ **c.** $x = 43°$

5. Yes, the parallelogram could have two angles with measure 54° and two angles with measure 126° for an angle sum of exactly 360°.

6. **a.** Ted's estimate is too large. The side must have a length less than $7 + 3.5 = 10.5$.

   b. Felicia's estimate is too small. The side must have a length greater than 7 because the side opposite the largest angle must be the longest side.

   c. Students' estimates should be greater than 7 but less than 10.5 .

7. 11 and 10

8. No, the sum of the angles is $34° + 45° + 100° = 179°$. A triangle has an angle sum of exactly 180°.

9. $m\angle 1 = 90°, m\angle 2 = 60°, m\angle 3 = 30°, m\angle 4 = 135°, m\angle 5 = 45°$.

10. **a.** Parallelogram

    b. The total distance around the parallelogram is 420 turtle steps.

    c. Two angles measure 60° and two angles measure 120°.

The Unit Project for *Shapes and Designs* is the What I Know About Shapes and Designs project. This project is introduced at the beginning of the student edition and formally assigned after Investigation 6. A possible scoring rubric and a sample from a student project are given here.

Suggested Scoring Rubric

This rubric for scoring the What I Know About Shapes and Designs project employs a scale that runs from 0 to 4, with a 4+ for work that goes beyond what has been asked for in some unique way. You may use this rubric as presented here or modify it to fit your district's requirements for evaluating and reporting students' work and understanding.

4+ Exemplary Response
- Complete, with clear, coherent explanations
- Shows understanding of the mathematical concepts and procedures
- Satisfies all essential conditions of the problem and goes beyond what is asked for in some unique way

4 Complete Response
- Complete, with clear, coherent explanations
- Shows understanding of the mathematical concepts and procedures
- Satisfies all essential conditions of the problem

3 Reasonably Complete Response
- Reasonably complete; may lack detail in explanations
- Shows understanding of most of the mathematical concepts and procedures
- Satisfies most of the essential conditions of the problem

2 Partial Response
- Gives response; explanation may be unclear or lack detail
- Shows some understanding of some of the mathematical concepts and procedures
- Satisfies some essential conditions of the problem

1 Inadequate Response
- Incomplete; explanation is insufficient or not understandable
- Shows little understanding of the mathematical concepts and procedures
- Fails to address essential conditions of the problem

0 No Attempt
- Irrelevant response
- Does not attempt a solution
- Does not address conditions of the problem

Sample Student Project

As her project, one student chose to make a book about shapes. Here are some excerpts from her project.

I͏t probably would be easier to tessellate a non-regular triangle by labeling the corners A, B, C.

TESSELATION POINT

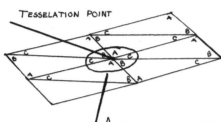

A triangle has to have 6 to a point, so instead of A, B, C, D, a *three* sided figure has to have A, A, B, B, C, C to a point.

USES FOR A TRIANGLE

T͏riangles are mostly used as supports for buildings, houses, scaffelings, ect. Quadrilaterals are not as sturdy as triangles because the corners of a quadrilateral can bend or lean over one way when you put pressure on it. W͏hen you put pressure on a triangle, it stays in a perfect triangle shape.

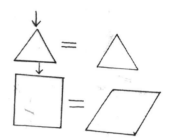

DIVIDING SHAPES INTO TRIANGLES

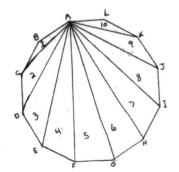

T͏his is a regular 12-sided dodecagon. F͏rom starting at point A and drawing a line to every corner, I began to form 10 triangles.

FAMILIAR TRIANGLES YOU USUALLY SEE

1. A Rooftop

2. Kitchen Knife

3. Clockhands

4. Ice-Cream Cone

Blackline Masters

Four in a Row Game Boards

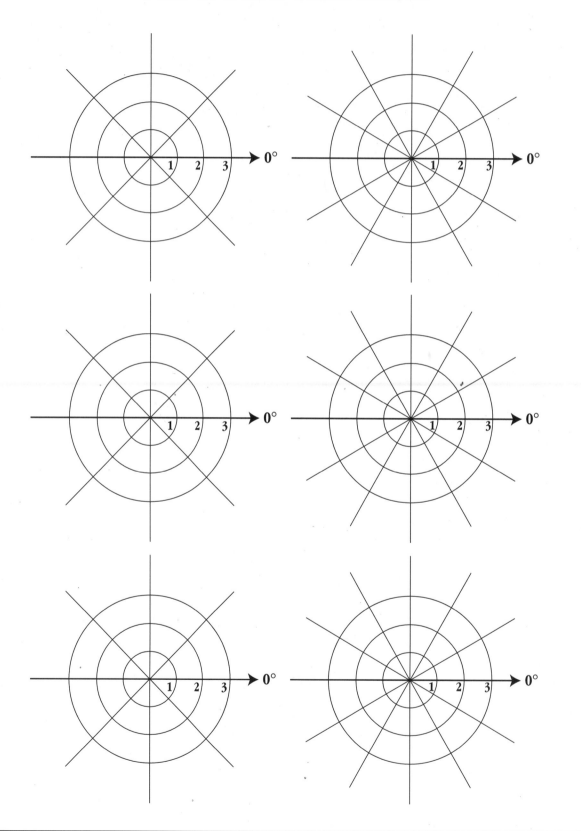

Angles and Polygons

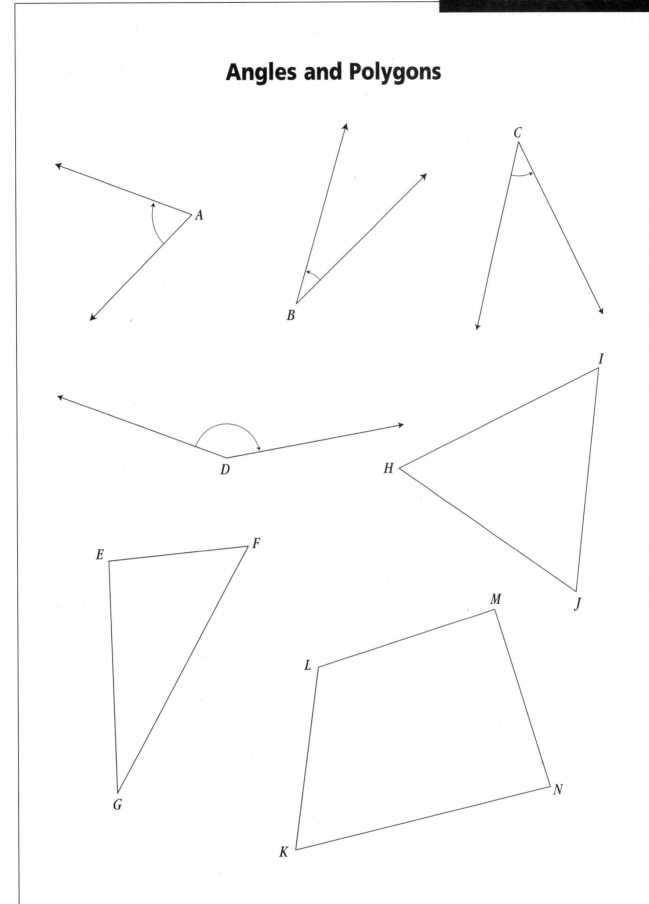

Sheet of Angles

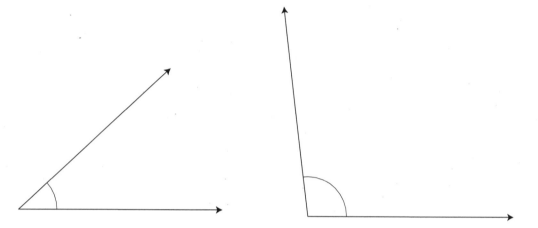

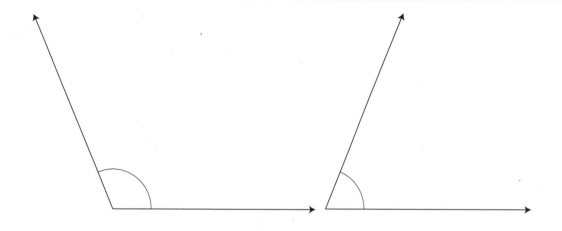

Irregular Polygons

1

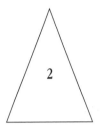

2

3

4

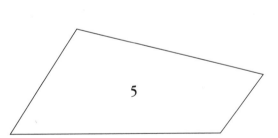

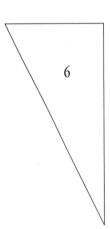

5

6

Polygons

Not Polygons

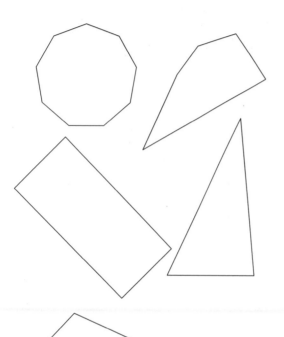

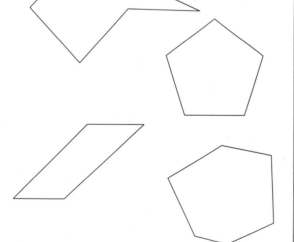

Line Symmetry

Turn Symmetry

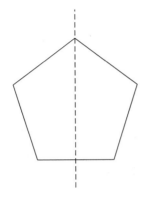

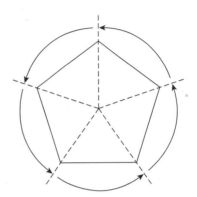

A polygon with line symmetry has two halves that are mirror images of each other.

A polygon with turn symmetry can be turned around its centerpoint and look the same at certain angles of rotation.

Tiling means covering a flat surface with shapes that fit together without any gaps. Which of the regular polygons shown below will tile a flat surface?

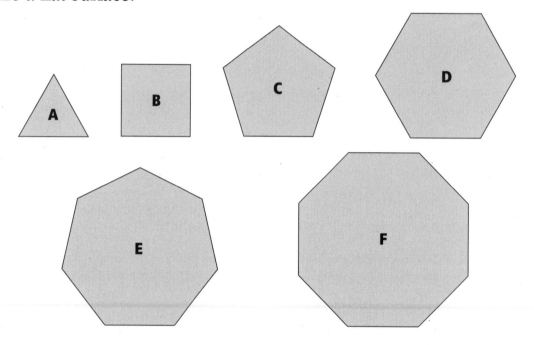

Use shapes A–F from your ShapeSet or cutouts of the shapes shown above to explore this question. As you work, try to figure out why some shapes cover a space, while others do not. Consider two types of tilings:

A. Patterns in which all the tiles are the same

B. Patterns that combine two or more different tiles

As you experiment, make sketches to share with your classmates. Keep a record of shapes and combinations of shapes that cover a surface and those that do not.

Suppose you are given three numbers to be lengths of sides in a triangle.

A. Will it always be possible to make a triangle with those side lengths?

B. Can you make two or more different triangles from the same side lengths?

Explore these questions by first selecting three numbers between 1 and 20 and then using polystrips to try to make a triangle with the numbers as side lengths. Repeat this several times with many different sets of three numbers. Sketch and label your results so you can share them with the class.

A good way to select numbers is to use number cubes. Toss three cubes, and use their sum as the length of one side. Toss the cubes two more times to get lengths for the other two sides.

Suppose you are given four numbers to be lengths of sides in a quadrilateral.

A. Will it always be possible to make a quadrilateral with those side lengths?

B. Can you make two or more different quadrilaterals from the same side lengths?

Explore these questions by first selecting four numbers between 1 and 20 and then using polystrips to try to make a quadrilateral with the numbers as side lengths. Repeat this several times with many different sets of four numbers. Sketch and label your results so you can share them with the class.

A good way to select numbers is to use number cubes. Toss three cubes, and use their sum as the length of one side. Toss the cubes three more times to get lengths for the other three sides.

The ten quadrilaterals shown below are examples of **parallelograms.** The name *parallelogram* is based on the word *parallel.* Parallel lines are straight lines that never meet, no matter how far they are extended.

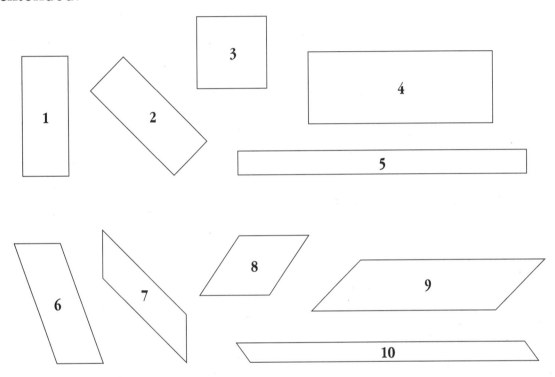

A. What do these ten quadrilaterals have in common that makes the name *parallelogram* sensible?

B. How do rectangles 1–5 differ from shapes 6–10 (which were formed by pressing on the corners of 1–5)?

C. How are the lengths of the sides of a parallelogram related?

Explore these questions by making a variety of parallelograms with polystrips. Sketch the results so you can share them with the class.

Look around your school, your home, and the other buildings and landscapes you see around you to find examples of angles. Find at least one example of each type of angle described.

A. An angle that occurs as the result of a *turning motion,* such as the opening of a door

B. An angle that occurs as a *wedge,* such as a piece of pizza

C. An angle that occurs as *two sides* with a *common vertex,* such as the branches on a tree

Explain where you found each angle, and make a sketch of the figure in which each angle appears. Be ready to share your findings with the class.

Sketch and find the degree measures of the angles made by these turns. For each sketch, include an arrow indicating the angle of turn.

A. One third of a right-angle turn

B. Two thirds of a right-angle turn

C. One quarter of a right-angle turn

D. One and one half right-angle turns

E. Two right-angle turns

F. Three right-angle turns

The angle below has a measure of about 120°. In G–L, make sketches of angles with *approximately* the given measure. For each sketch, include an arrow indicating the angle of turn.

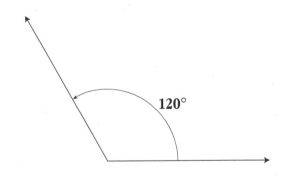

G. 20°

H. 70°

I. 150°

J. 180°

K. 270°

L. 360°

A.

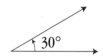

30°

B.

60°

C.

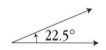

22.5°

D.

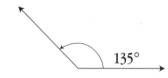

135°

E.

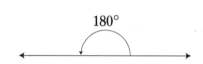

180°

F.

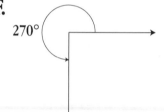

270°

G.

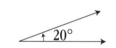

20°

H.

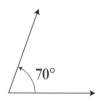

70°

I.

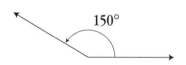

150°

J.

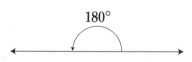

180°

K.

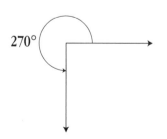

270°

L.

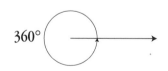

360°

Estimate and record the measure of each angle of shapes A, B, D, M, R, and, V in your ShapeSet. Copy the shapes onto a sheet of paper, and label each angle with its measure.

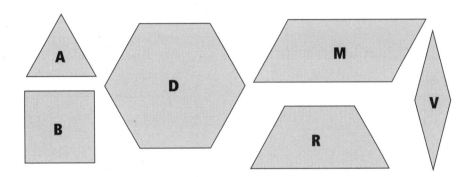

Play Four in a Row several times. Play games with both the 30° grid and the 45° grid on Labsheet 3.4. Write down any winning strategies you discover.

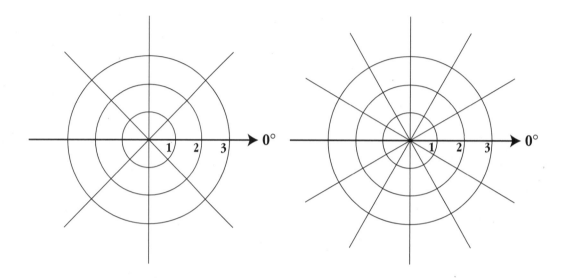

Measure each angle of shapes A, B, D, M, R, and V in your ShapeSet. Copy the shapes onto a sheet of paper, and label each angle with its measure. Use your results to answer the questions below.

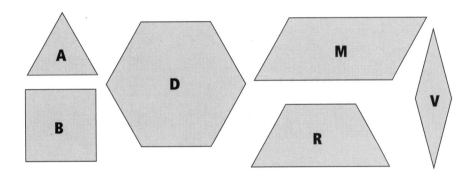

A. How do your measures with the angle ruler compare with your estimates from Problem 3.3?

B. Where do you find two or more angles of the same size in the same shape?

C. Where do you find two or more angles of the same size in different shapes?

D. What combinations of the six shapes pictured above will work together to make a tiling? What patterns do you see in the angles of these shapes?

How many degrees off course was Earhart's crash site from her intended destination?

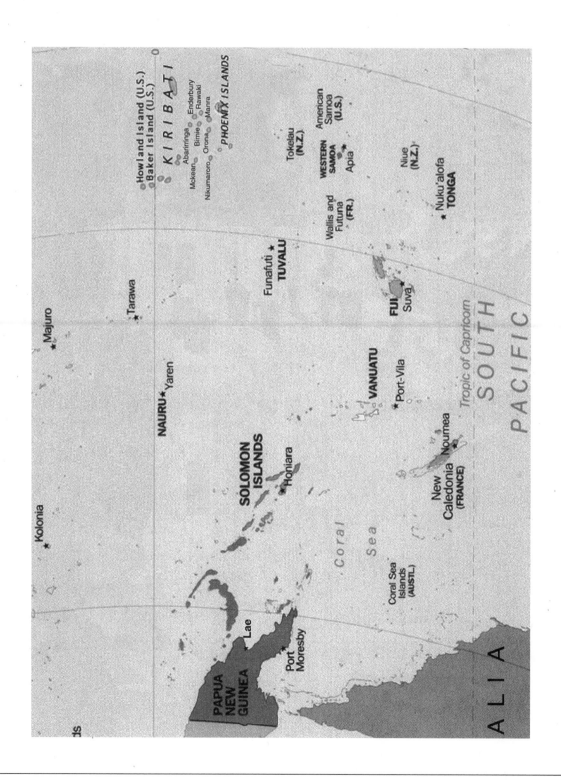

Count the sides of each of these six regular polygons. Measure the interior angles with your angle ruler.

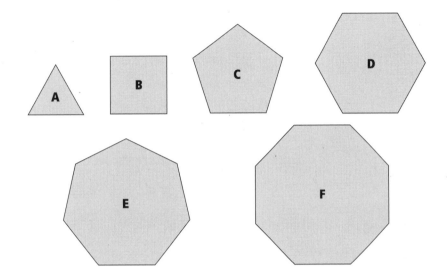

A. Make a table that shows the name of each polygon, the number of sides it has, the measure of each of its angles, and the sum of the measures of all of its angles (this is called the *angle sum*).

B. In your table, look for patterns that relate the number of sides a polygon has to the measure of its angles and to its angle sum. Think about ways to complete these statements:

- If a regular polygon has _____ sides, the angle sum of the polygon is _____ degrees.

- If a regular polygon has _____ sides, each angle measures _____ degrees.

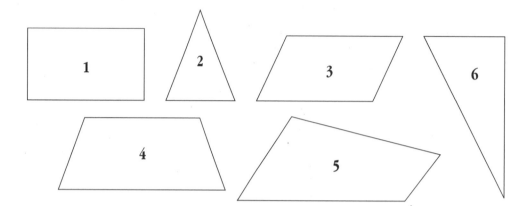

A. For each triangle and quadrilateral shown above, measure each interior angle and compute the angle sum.

B. How do the angle sums for these irregular polygons compare with the angle sums for the regular polygons?

C. Test the side-angle patterns you found by measuring the interior angles of some other triangles and quadrilaterals from your ShapeSet.

D. Use the information you have discovered about triangles and quadrilaterals to make a guess about the angle sums in irregular pentagons and hexagons. Test your guess by drawing and measuring some irregular pentagons and hexagons.

Explore tilings made from a single type of regular polygon. Consider patterns with triangles only, squares only, pentagons only, hexagons only, heptagons only, and octagons only. Make sketches to show what you discover.

A. Which regular polygons fit around a vertex point exactly? What are the angle measures of these polygons?

B. Which regular polygons do not fit around a point exactly? What are the angle measures of these polygons?

C. What seems to be the key that tells which regular polygons will fit together in a tiling and which will not?

A. In the tiling of equilateral triangles, describe all the different ways the shape can be placed in the hole. How many ways are there in all?

B. In the tiling of isosceles triangles, describe all the different ways the shape can be placed in the hole. Is the number of ways you can put the isosceles triangle in the hole less than, greater than, or equal to the number of ways you can put the equilateral triangle in the hole? Explain.

You may find it helpful to use your ShapeSet to investigate the different ways you can flip and turn the triangle. Use the numbers on the vertices of the triangles to help you describe how each triangle can be flipped and turned to position it in the hole in different ways.

A. In the tiling of squares, describe all the different ways the shape can be placed in the hole. How many ways are there in all?

B. In the tiling of rectangles, describe all the different ways the shape can be placed in the hole. How many ways are there in all?

C. In tiling of parallelograms, describe all the different ways the shape can be placed in the hole. How many ways are there in all?

You may find it helpful to use your ShapeSet to investigate the different ways you can flip and turn the shapes. Use the numbers on the vertices of the shapes to help you describe how each shape can be flipped and turned to position it in the hole in different ways.

Spend some time exploring the kinds of shapes and designs you can make with combinations of Logo commands. For example, you might try to draw letters or designs like those below. Try writing commands to draw the initials of your name.

In this problem, you will write a Logo computer program to draw a triangle. Follow these steps:

■ On a piece of paper, write a Logo program that you think will draw a triangle.

■ Type your Logo program into the computer.

■ Debug your program. Keep making changes in your program until you have produced a triangle.

■ Write down your new, debugged program for drawing a triangle.

Write Logo programs to make each of the following shapes. Experiment at the computer to test and debug your programs. Each shape can be made in lots of different ways.

A. A square with sides of length 50

B. A rectangle with sides of length 50 and 100

C. A parallelogram—but not a rectangle—with sides of length 80 and 30

D. A parallelogram—but not a square—with all sides of length 70

Dear Family,

The next unit in your child's course of study in mathematics class this year is *Shapes and Designs*. Its focus is geometry, and it teaches students about some properties of shapes and some relationships between shapes. The unit engages students in a series of activities that allow them to discover many of the key properties of polygons and how these properties make such shapes useful. This is the first unit in *Connected Mathematics* on geometry. The unit goals include developing the ability to recognize and analyze shapes and to measure the sides and angles of various shapes.

As part of the assessment for this unit, your child will be asked to do a project on the common polygons studied in the unit: triangles, squares, rectangles, parallelograms, quadrilaterals, pentagons, hexagons, and octagons. Throughout the unit, students will be recording what they learn about each polygon (its properties) and describing how the polygons relate to each other. Students will also be looking for places where these different shapes can be found in their world.

You can help your child see how this part of geometry is important in everyday life in several ways:

- When you are with your child, perhaps walking through a mall or a park, point out different shapes you see, and ask your child to find other shapes.

- Whenever you notice an interesting shape in a newspaper or a magazine, discuss with your child whether it is one of the polygons mentioned above, and suggest that it might be cut out and saved for the shapes project.

- Have your child share his or her mathematics notebook with you, showing you what has been recorded about the different shapes being studied. Ask your child to explain why these ideas are important, and try to share ways that shapes help you with work or hobbies.

- Look over your child's homework and make sure all questions are answered and that explanations are clear.

As always, if you have any questions or concerns about geometry or your child's progress in the class, please feel free to call. All of us here are interested in your child and want to be sure that this year's mathematics experiences are enjoyable and promote a firm understanding of mathematics.

Sincerely,

Estimada familia,

La próxima unidad del programa de matemáticas de su hijo o hija para este curso se llama *Shapes and Designs* (*Figuras, formas y diseños*). La misma trata principalmente sobre la geometrìa, y en ella los alumnos estudian algunas propiedades de las figuras y algunas relaciones existentes entre ellas. Además, participan en una serie de actividades en las que descubren muchas de las propiedades clave de los polìgonos y las maneras en que dichas propiedades hacen de éstos figuras útiles. Se trata de la primera unidad de geometrìa de *Connected Mathematics*. En ella se intenta crear la capacidad para identificar y analizar figuras y medir los lados y los ángulos de diversas figuras.

Como parte de la evaluación de esta unidad, a su hijo o hija se le pedirá que realice un proyecto sobre los polígonos más típicos de la misma: triángulos, cuadrados, rectángulos, paralelogramos, cuadriláteros, pentágonos, hexágonos y octágonos. A lo largo de la unidad, anotará lo que aprenda sobre cada polígono (sus propiedades) y describirá cómo todos ellos están relacionados entre sí. Además, buscará en el entorno que le rodea lugares en los que las distintas figuras puedan encontrarse.

Para ayudar a su hijo o hija a comprender cómo estos aspectos de la geometría son importantes en la vida diaria, ustedes pueden hacer lo siguiente:

- Cuando estén con su hijo o hija como, por ejemplo, en un centro comercial o en un parque, señálenle las distintas figuras que observen y pídanle que busque otras.

- Cuando observen en un periódico o en una revista una figura interesante, comenten con su hijo o hija acerca de si se trata de uno de los polígonos ya mencionados y recomiéndenle que la recorte y guarde para el proyecto de figuras.

- Pídanle que comparta con ustedes su cuaderno de matemáticas y que les muestre sus anotaciones sobre las distintas figuras tratadas. Díganle que les explique por qué dichas anotaciones son importantes y hablen con él o ella sobre las maneras en que las figuras facilitan el trabajo o los pasatiempos.

- Repasen su tarea para asegurarse de que conteste todas las preguntas y escriba con claridad las explicaciones.

Y como de costumbre, si ustedes necesitan más detalles o aclaraciones respecto a la geometría o sobre los progresos de su hijo o hija en esta clase, no duden en llamarnos. A todos nos interesa su hijo o hija y queremos asegurarnos de que las experiencias matemáticas que tenga este año sean lo más amenas posibles y ayuden a fomentar en él o ella una sólida comprensión de las matemáticas.

Atentamente,

Isometric Dot Paper

ShapeSet

To make a complete ShapeSet, make eight copies of this page and the following page.

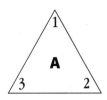
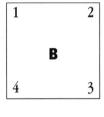
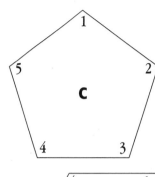
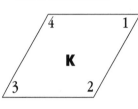
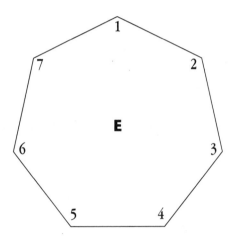
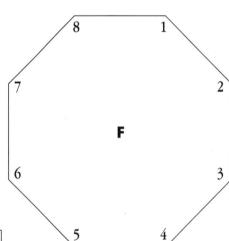
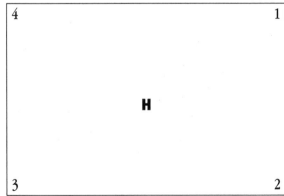
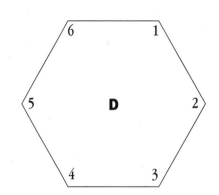

Shapes and Designs

To make a complete ShapeSet, make eight copies of this page and the previous page.

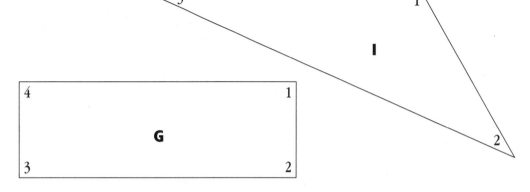

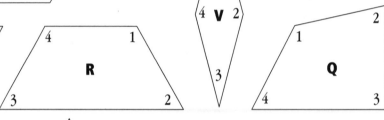

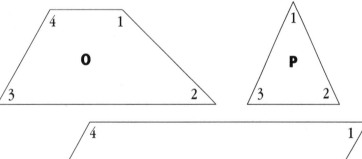

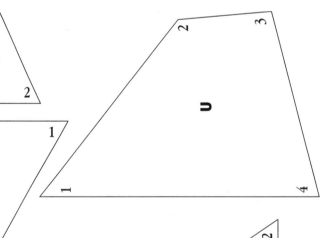

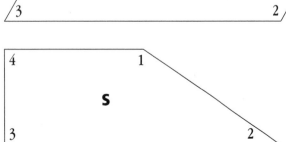

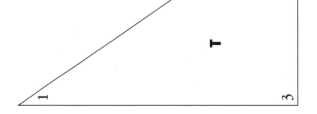

A Polystrip set contains six strips of each length.

Additional Practice

Investigation 1

Answer parts a and b for each polygon below.

1.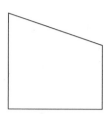

2.

3.

4.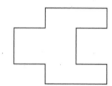

5.

6.

   a. Is the shape a regular polygon? Explain why or why not.

   b. Could the shape be used to tile a surface? Make a sketch to demonstrate your answer.

7. The shape below is composed of four polygons.

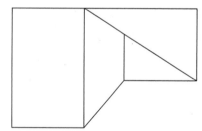

   a. Describe the four polygons in the shape.

   b. Can the shape be used to tile a surface? Make a sketch to demonstrate your answer.

Investigation 2

1. A quadrilateral has two sides of length 6. The sum of the lengths of the other two sides is 15. Use this information to answer the following questions.

   a. Suppose the two sides of length 6 are adjacent to each other. What might the lengths of the other two sides be? Explain your reasoning.

   b. Suppose the quadrilateral is a rectangle and the two sides of length 6 are opposite each other. What would the lengths of the other two sides have to be? Explain how you found your answer.

   c. Could the quadrilateral have two sides of length 6, one side of length 13.5, and one side of length 1.5? Explain why or why not.

2. Bob has sketched an equilateral triangle. The sum of the lengths of the sides is 11.5. What is the length of each side of Bob's triangle? Explain your reasoning.

3. Angela has sketched a rectangle. She says that the lengths of the sides of the rectangle add to 26, and the length of one side is 7. What are the length and width of Angela's rectangle? Explain how you found your answer.

4. Use the triangle below to answer the following questions.

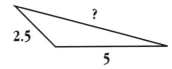

   a. Alex estimates that the unknown side length is about 4.5. How do you think Alex's estimate compares with the actual length? Explain your reasoning.

   b. Jennifer estimates that the unknown side length is about 8. How do you think Jennifer's estimate compares with the actual length? Explain your reasoning.

   c. Use what you have learned about making triangles with polystrips to estimate the length of the unknown side. Explain why you think your estimate is close to the actual length.

Investigation 3

1. Use the circular grid below to answer the following questions.

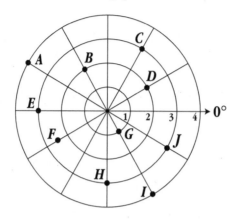

a. Find the (distance, angle measure) coordinates for points A through J.

b. What is the distance from point A to point J? Explain how you found your answer.

c. What is the distance from point F to point D?

d. What is the distance from point B to point I?

e. What is the measure of the angle with vertex at the origin and sides that pass through points H and J? Explain how you found your answer.

f. What is the measure of the angle with vertex at the origin and sides that pass through points A and I?

2. Use the diagram of the polygon shown below to answer the following questions.

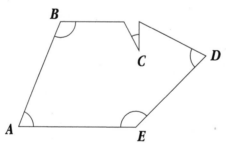

a. Estimate the measures of angles A through E.

b. Use your angle ruler to find the measure of each angle. How do the measures compare with your estimates from part a?

c. Is the polygon a regular polygon? Why or why not?

Investigation 4

1. An isosceles triangle has two 50° angles. What is the measure of the third angle? Explain how you found your answer.

2. One angle of an isosceles triangle measures 100°. What are the measures of the other two angles? Explain your reasoning.

3. Two of the angles of a parallelogram measure 75°. What are the measures of the other two angles? Explain your reasoning.

4. One angle of a parallelogram measures 40° and another angle measures 140°. What are the measures of the other two angles? Explain how you found your answer.

5. Can a parallelogram have two 45° angles and two 75° angles? Why or why not?

6. For each of the shapes below, find the unknown angle measure without using your angle ruler.

a.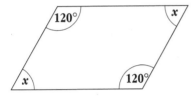

b.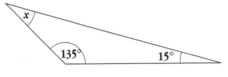

c.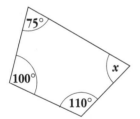

d.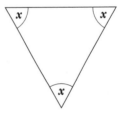

Investigation 5

1. At right is a diagram of Ms. Lichtman's classroom. Students sit at identical rectangular tables. Use the diagram and what you know about side relationships to answer the following questions.

   a. If you were to trace your finger around one of the tables, what total distance would your finger travel?

   b. Ms. Lichtman is planning to put a strip of masking tape around the edges of each table so that papers and pencils won't slide off as easily. What is the total length of the masking tape Ms. Lichtman will need?

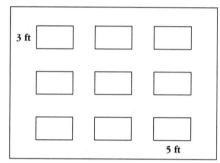

Front of Classroom

2. Use the design at right and what you know about angle relationships to answer the following questions.

   a. If the measure of angle 1 is 25°, what is the measure of angle 2? Explain your reasoning.

   b. If the measure of angle 1 is 25°, what is the measure of angle 3? Explain your reasoning.

   c. What is the measure of angle 4? Explain your reasoning

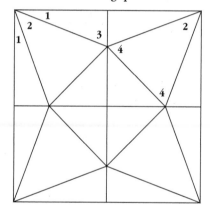

3. Use the diagram at right and what you know about angle relationships to answer the following questions.

   a. What is the measure of angle 3?

   b. The measure of angle 1 is one-fourth of the measure of angle 3. What is the measure of angle 1?

   c. What is the measure of angle 2?

   d. The measure of angle 4 is twice the measure of angle 1. What is the measure of angle 4?

   e. What is the measure of angle 5?

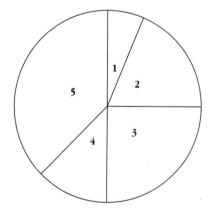

Investigation 6

1. Write a Logo program that will draw an equilateral triangle. Remember that an equilateral triangle has three equal angles and three equal sides.

2. The Logo program below is supposed to draw a rectangle with two sides of length 75 turtle steps and two sides of length 150 turtle steps. Unfortunately, the program has two errors in it. Find and correct both errors.

```
fd 75
lt 90
fd 150
lt 90
fd 150
rt 180
fd 150
```

3. Refer to the Logo program below to answer the following questions.

```
fd 100
rt 90
fd 200
rt 90
fd 100
rt 90
fd 200
```

   a. What shape does this program create?

   b. How many steps does it take the turtle to trace out the figure?

   c. What is the sum of all the interior angles of the figure?

© Dale Seymour Publications®

Answer Keys

Investigation 1

1–6. **a.** None of the shapes are regular polygons because none contain sides and angles that are all the same size.

    b. Only the circle, shape 6, cannot be used to tile a surface. Drawings will vary.

7. **a.** The shape contains a rectangle, a small triangle, a large triangle, and a quadrilateral.

    b. The shape can tile a surface. Drawings will vary.

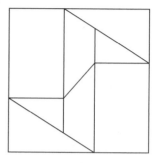

Investigation 2

1. **a.** Each side would have a length of 7.5.

    b. Possible answers: 5 and 10, 3 and 12, 7 and 8

    c. No; the sum of any three sides must be greater than the length of the fourth side. In this case, the sum of the three shortest sides, $1.5 + 6 + 6 = 13.5$, is not greater than the fourth side, 13.5.

2. Each side length would be 11.5 divided by 3, or 3.5.

3. One pair of sides would have length 7, and the other pair would have length 6.

4. **a.** Alex's estimate is too small. The longest side should be more than 5 (the length of one of the two shorter sides).

    b. Jennifer's estimate is too large. The length of the side must be less than $2.5 + 5 = 7.5$.

    c. Answers will vary but should be greater than 5 and less than 7.5.

Investigation 3

1. **a.** $A = (4, 150°)$, $B = (2, 120°)$, $C = (3, 60°)$, $D = (2, 30°)$, $E = (3, 180°)$, $F = (2.5, 210°)$, $G = (1, 300°)$, $H = (3, 270°)$, $I = (4, 300°)$, $J = (3, 330°)$.

    b. 7   **c.** 4.5   **d.** 6

    e. 60°   **f.** 150°

2. **a–b.** A is about 75°, B is about 105°, C is about 30°, D is about 75°, E is about 135°.

    c. No; All angles and sides are not equal.

Investigation 4

1. Since the sum of the angles must be 180°, the third angle must have a measure of 80°.

2. An isosceles triangle has two equal angles. These two angles can't each measure 100° because the total of all three angles must be 180°. Therefore, the two equal angles must add to 80°, so they must measure 40° each.

3. The measures of the other two angles must add to 210°, so each angle must measure 105°.

4. Since parallelograms have two pairs of equal angles, the other two angles must measure 140° and 40°.

5. No, because the sum of the angle measures is only 240°. The sum of the angle measures of a parallelogram must be 360°.

6. a. 60°   b. 30°   c. 75°   d. 60°

Investigation 5

1. a. 16 feet   b. 144 feet

2. a. $90° - 2(25°) = 90° - 50° = 40°$

   b. $180° - (90° + 25°) = 180° - 115° = 65°$

   c. $\frac{180° - 40°}{2} - 70°$

3. a. 90°   b. 22.5°   c. 67.5°   d. 45°

   e. 135°

Investigation 6

1. Answers will vary. The program below draws a triangle with sides of length 5.

```
lt 30
fd 50
lt 120
fd 50
lt 120
fd 50
```

2. Here is a copy of the program with the errors highlighted and corrected:

```
fd 75
lt 90
fd 150
lt 90
fd 150    Should be fd 75
rt 180    Should be rt 270 or lt 90
fd 150
```

3. a. rectangle   b. 600   c. 360°

angle The opening between two straight lines that meet at a vertex, measured in degrees or radians. The angle at point *A* on the triangle below is identified as angle *BAC* or ∠*BAC*.

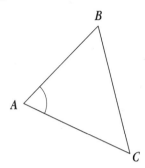

The sides of an angle are rays that have the vertex as a starting point. Each of the three angles below is formed by the joining of two rays.

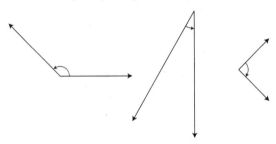

degree A unit of measure of angles equal to $\frac{1}{360}$ of complete circle. The angle below measures about 1°; 360 of these would just fit around a point and fill in a complete circle; 90 of them make a right angle.

1°

diagonal A line segment connecting two nonadjacent vertices of a polygon. All quadrilaterals have two diagonals, as shown below. The two diagonals of a square are equal in length, and the two diagonals of a rectangle are equal in length. A pentagon has five diagonals, and a hexagon has six diagonals.

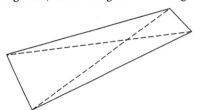

equilateral triangle A triangle with all three sides the same length.

isosceles triangle A triangle with two sides the same length.

parallel lines Lines that never meet no matter how long they are extended. The opposite sides of a regular hexagon are parallel. The polygons A and B below each have one pair of opposite sides parallel. In polygons C, D, and E, both pairs of opposite sides are parallel.

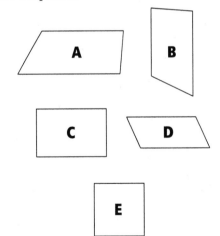

parallelogram A quadrilateral in which both pairs of opposite sides are equal and parallel. Both pairs of opposite angles are also equal. Figure D in the definition of parallel lines on the previous page, as well as rectangle C and square E, are all parallelograms.

polygon A closed, flat (two-dimensional) shape whose sides are formed by line segments. Below are examples of two polygons, a hexagon and a pentagon.

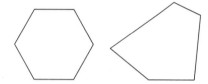

Special polygon names are derived from Greek prefixes that tell the number of sides or the number of angles in the polygon.

- *triangle:* 3 sides and angles
- *quadrilateral:* 4 sides and angles
- *pentagon:* 5 sides and angles
- *hexagon:* 6 sides and angles
- *heptagon:* 7 sides and angles
- *octagon:* 8 sides and angles
- *nonagon* (also called *enneagon*): 9 sides and angles
- *decagon:* 10 sides and angles
- *dodecagon:* 12 sides and angles

properties of shapes Characteristics of shapes that are always valid. For example, you have learned that a property of parallelograms is that they have two pairs of parallel sides. The sum of the angles of a 6-sided polygon is $180° \times 4$ or $720°$. Triangles are stable figures, since their shape is completely determined by the lengths of their sides.

quadrilateral A polygon with four sides. Below are two quadrilaterals.

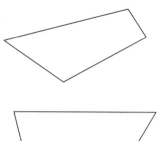

rectangle A parallelogram with all right angles, as shown below. Squares are a special type of rectangle.

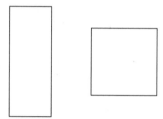

regular polygon A polygon that has all of its sides equal and all of its angles equal. The hexagon below is regular, but the pentagon is not regular, because its sides and its angles are not equal.

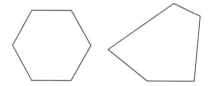

right angle An angle that measures $90°$. All of the vertices in a rectangle, such as the one below, are right angles.

rhombus A quadrilateral that has all sides the same length.

side One of the line segments that make up the boundaries of a polygon.

square A rectangle with all sides equal. Thus squares have four right angles and four equal sides.

tiling Also called a tessellation. The filling of a plane surface with geometric shapes without gaps or overlaps. These shapes are usually regular polygons or other common polygons. The tiling below is made of triangles. You could remove some of the line segments to create a tiling of parallelograms, or remove still more to create a tiling of hexagons. In a tiling, a vertex is a point where the corners of the polygons fit together.

trapezoid A quadrilateral with one pair of opposite sides parallel. This definition means that parallelograms are trapezoids. The figures below are all trapezoids.

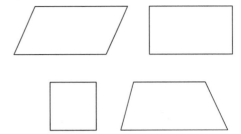

vertex The corners of a polygon. For example, *G, H, I, J,* and *K* are all vertices in the pentagon below. All angles have vertices; for example, in the hexagon below, angle *AFE* has a vertex at *F.*

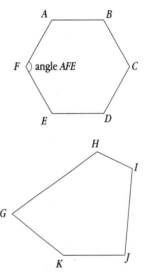

Index

Index

Index